WRITING
RESEARCH PAPERS
with
CONFIDENCE

Student Edition

Sheila Moss

PUBLISHING GROUP

NASHVILLE, TENNESSEE

10-digit ISBN: 0805443649
13-digit ISBN: 9780805443646

Published by Broadman & Holman Publishers
Nashville, Tennessee

DEWEY: 808
SUBHD: REPORT WRITING / RESEARCH:

2 3 4 5 6 7   13 12 11 10 09 08

CONTENTS

SCOPE AND SEQUENCE

SCOPE
AND
SEQUENCE

v

SCOPE
AND
SEQUENCE

ACKNOWLEDGMENTS

Acknowledging how a project comes to fruition is more complicated than it seems if one takes seriously all that has gone into its compilation. For those of us who believe in the Lord Jesus Christ who begins a good work in us and carries it to completion until His day, the good work is, of course, our salvation, found in no other than Himself. I often wonder, though, if the good work He begins in us goes beyond salvation to include those tasks He leads us to throughout our lives. If that truly is the case, then I can confidently say He has brought me to this point in my life: He prepared the way, initiated, and led the development of this study, resulting from experiences He has taken me through. I believe the study's primary purpose is to help prepare our children for deeper levels of thinking through the processes of researching and writing. He brought me to this point of writing it, and He brought you to this point of considering it for your students. To Him belongs whatever honor is associated with both.

There are always people who help us along the way. When Matt Stewart and I batted around the idea of finding a writing text for the high school homeschool community, Matt ultimately challenged "How about just writing it yourself." I argued *Lack of time!* but Matt wasn't deterred. We toyed with the idea and then got serious about it. Consulting Zan Tyler was a bonus since she had insights into specific needs for the homeschool community, and those insights agreed with a research program to stimulate excellence in writing. After she expressed excitement about my curriculum proposal, I moved on to discovering the perceived writing needs in the homeschool community and chatting informally with friends and family who teach high schoolers at home. Pam Braswell at Broadman & Holman patiently fielded questions and shuffled manuscripts back and forth. I've also been honored with tips and experiences from Christ Presbyterian Academy: Principal Phil Boeing has been a friendly counselor and academician-par excellence for my family for years and has readily availed his teachers and staff to me. Alice Jones-Toledo, Laura Pollock, and Joy MacKenzie gladly shared some of their techniques and research procedures, while Beverly Payne and Marsha Wilson coached me about the Questia computer program for research.

Then, there are supporters who listened, responded, challenged, encouraged, and read portions of the manuscript in progress (Shelia T., Trish,

Sharon, and Margaret); dear souls who willingly, even eagerly, shared their former writings for samples and examples (Gretchen and Judson); and children who asked over and over "How's it going, Mom?" (Milton, Chimena, Vanessa, Cameron, and Gretchen).

Every writer needs a really good editor, and I've been blessed with two—an informal one early on who patiently read through my rough ideas and offered suggestions and comments (Gretchen) and my official one who has read with a "fine-toothed comb" to catch my inconsistencies and odd structures (Chimena). Thanks, ladies; recognizing you as the true writers, I've leaned heavily not only on your expertise but also on your encouragement. Working professionally with daughters gives new depth to *family* and reverses the "margin dots" technique we devised years ago!

LESSON ONE

INTRODUCING *WRITING RESEARCH PAPERS*

Thesis: In Writing Research Papers with Confidence students practice and implement higher-level thinking skills as they systematically plan, investigate, record, assimilate, and write about a subject or question.

**Lesson One
Overview**

A. Concepts

1. Lesson overview

2. Background

3. Reasons for research

4. Library familiarity

5. Writing and thinking

6. Higher-level thinking skills

   a. Knowledge dimensions

   b. Cognitive process dimensions

B. Assignments

1. Preparation for research

2. Research portfolio

3. Research language: *knowledge dimensions, cognitive process dimensions, on-line, card catalog, Dewey Decimal System, Library of Congress System, computerized catalog, electronic databases, CD-ROM, research, communication, style, essay, library, reference, source, write*

4. Collaborative learning interview: professional librarian

5. Evaluations

6. SAT preparation prompts: grammar, diction, and usage— identifying sentence errors; essay writing

7. Sample essays

CONCEPTS

INTRODUCTION TO *WRITING RESEARCH PAPERS*

Background

Some people solve mysteries; some work puzzles. Others favor adventure and exploration while still others prefer a journey, a quest, or a discovery. Mysteries, puzzles, adventures, explorations, journeys, quests, and discoveries are *metaphors* (images or descriptions) for what *writing research papers* can become for you. If you are already acquainted with the phenomenon of research, you've developed an attitude and opinion about it. Hopefully, your position is pleasant enough not to thwart you from a new adventure with it. If you have never experienced formal research, you can approach the venture with an unclouded vision and with positive expectations. You will not have to overcome preconceived notions that could prevent you from experiencing the research process with the most positive outlook. If you have accomplished research before, you know that it requires hard work and tenacity. Whether you have or haven't done research, rest assured that the hard work and tenacity can be guided in such a way as to make the task very manageable. Additionally, you can approach research with confidence as you follow these carefully designed procedures.

Why Bother? Reasons for Research

My job is to guide you through the research process. We will use standard systematic procedures known throughout the research community. However, they will be geared to your particular level of expertise, your particular circumstances, and your particular time constraints. You and your educator will make decisions and choices about all three—expertise, circumstances, and constraints. You will know what is expected at all times; you will have a voice in what you are doing; and you will evaluate your progress along the way so there will be no surprises at the end of the project. How well I lead will partially determine your research success. Another part of your success will be determined by your educator, but the most crucial part of your success is determined by you. You are the most important element of any paper that comes through your intellect and your pen. It is *your* signature that assures readers of the validity of your research. When you present your research to your reading public, *your* name authenticates your work, which becomes a part of your academic, business, home, and community reputation. What a challenge, what a privilege, and what a responsibility to know that you influence the thinking of your readership!

Before your academic research actually begins, realize that research is something you are already acquainted with in daily living—you do it every day without even thinking about it. When you decide you need a new outfit, you probably look around in several stores, compare prices and sizes and styles, try on several for just the right look, evaluate all the information against the amount of money in your pocket, and then decide if this outfit is the one you really want, if it fits the occasion, and if your friends like it, too. Sometimes a lot of thought and time goes into the final decision. You may even discover you have to start over when the very outfit you want isn't available in the color you prefer. You either adjust your expectations or continue your search by going to another shopping mall. When you make these plans and decisions, you are actually doing research to find the solution to a question or a problem: Where can I find an outfit at the best price in my size and special color for this particular event? You are on a mission, an act of discovery; you explore your options, fit the puzzle pieces together, and solve the mystery while you're on the adventure. That's what academic research is, and that's similar to what it takes to accomplish it: planning, discovery, exploring, questioning, comparing, analyzing, adjusting, evaluating, and solving: the procedures and metaphor possibilities go on and on.

Consider another research challenge: the importance of and reasons for doing research. Many students enter the research process totally convinced that since nothing about academic research can be beneficial to them, devoting time and effort to such picky details is a waste. Typically, students have heard older folks say something like, "You'll need to know this in the future; you'll have to know this when you go to college; you'll need to know how to do this when you go out into the world, when you get a job, when you . . . ." Somewhere along the way you probably either stopped listening or became weary of that reasoning. Check out the following practical scenario.

You may be in the season of life where you're thinking about going to college or getting a really good job or planning a career. If it's college, you may have the option to go wherever you want because you have excellent grades, unlimited funds, or are in the *legacy* category because all your important relatives have gone to prestigious universities; plus, dignitaries know you, vouch for you, and can get you in wherever you want to go. In that case, perhaps researching several colleges is not necessary, and you won't actually need to do research about your options. However, if that scenario isn't totally factual, you may need to search for colleges in your academic range, your price range, and your locale so that securing a place in a freshman class becomes reality.

How and where do you begin if you have more than one option? Perhaps you ask yourself, "Would I rather go to Mid-State or Up-State or Eastern, or can I even go out of state? Christian college? Liberal Arts college? School of technology? What are the requirements? What academic programs do they offer? How much is tuition? Room and board? Books? What about transportation? What is the enrollment? Is enrollment open? Is there early admission? Are scholarships available? Is this a good college? What *is* a good college anyway?" You'll need to search for information to answer these questions. Where does the information come from? Should you depend on what your friend's brother's cousin says about the college in her town and let that determine your decision? Do you have the liberty of doing your own thinking and searching, or will someone else make the decision for you? Questions, decisions, searching; questions, decisions, more searching—you're on your way to what you can officially call *research*.

**Recording
Research**

But how do you keep up with all the information from all these colleges? How do you remember which ones have open enrollment and which ones have the most gorgeous campuses? In classes or businesses or life scenarios that require research, there is an added dimension to research—*the act of actually writing the findings in a standard presentable research form commonly accepted in research communities*. Why is that important? Why not just make a few notes and lists and then form an opinion? Why go to all the trouble to look through many books and journals and who knows what else? These questions are very important in the realm of research. The step of actually writing it is most valuable. *Writing* research has benefits for more people than you alone.

Suppose you decide that your research work could benefit other students. You may even be able to present it well enough to publish it and sell it to others who need the information. Suppose your parents or your business insists on knowing what you find out after you've done the exploring. They don't want to wade through scratchy handwriting jotted on bits of paper, and they want to know you did a very thorough job of research. Most likely their finances are involved, and they need accurate evidence that you know what you're talking about. Actually, they want to know if they should back you financially in the first place. They are looking for competence and maturity and exactness as well as answers to the initial questions. This is your time to shine, to win their support, to perhaps even reap the rewards of your diligence. You benefit personally because you have the results of your study, you know what was involved in answering the questions, and you have gained insight into what happens when others do comparable research. You've learned how to read more objectively, to evaluate what you read, and to better understand the material you've covered. You've developed a language for talking about colleges, what they require, your preferences, which arguments will be most convincing for the colleges on your narrowed-down list, and most importantly, what questions need to be asked. You've become familiar with significant decision-making processes and perhaps with the pleasure of solving your own questions. You have learned the standards associated with a specific community that expects diligence, accuracy, clarity, and above all validity, the kind of accomplishment you want in your life regardless of which direction you take. Who knows? You might even need this information in the future or when you go to college or when you get a job or when you . . . ! As you know, the preacher in Ecclesiastes says "there is no end to the making of many books, and much study wearies the body," so we need good reasons for doing the work that comes with the study of many books! (Ec 12:12 HCSB) Think about why you are researching and writing and what it can add to your studying of many books.

Research really isn't new to you; research is valuable; and writing research really has it rewards. Let's get started and discover the value and the rewards!

Library Familiarity

Unless you are already experienced in researched writing, you will be drawing heavily on the services of librarians. When you call for your first library tour, ask about orientation services and who is available to teach you the intricacies of the library. Since library science is the specialty of librarians, and they typically have a deep affinity for books, they are usually very helpful. While you are there, become familiar with the *on-line general catalogue*, the *card catalogue and computerized catalogs*, the *electronic databases*, and *reference works* (indexes, bibliographies, collections of abstracts, guides to research, dictionaries, atlases, etc.) in both print and electronic forms. Libraries use either the Dewey Decimal System to classify their books or the Library of Congress System. The former has ten major headings, and the later has twenty major headings; books are found in the stacks (shelves open to browsing), at the reserve desk (kept for in-library circulation only), or at the circulation desk (if the stacks are not open for browsing), according to their call number (designation by either Dewey Decimal or Library of Congress).

Dewey Decimal System		
	000	General works
	100	Philosophy and psychology
	200	Religion
	300	Social sciences
	400	Language
	500	Natural sciences and mathematics
	600	Technology and applied sciences
	700	Fine arts
	800	Literature
	900	Geography and history

Library of Congress System		
	A	General works
	B	Philosophy and psychology
	C	General history
	D	World history
	E-F	American history
	G	Geography and anthropology
	H	Social sciences
	J	Political science
	K	Law
	L	Education
	M	Music
	N	Fine arts
	P	Language and literature
	Q	Science
	R	Medicine
	S	Agriculture
	T	Technology
	U	Military science
	V	Naval science
	Z	Bibliography and library science

As you can see, the library is far more than a place that has books. The librarian can introduce you to library strategies with computer databases, either on-line or on CD-ROM. Since libraries use various systems for their computer catalogues, you'll need to consult your librarian to learn how to use the system to locate books and periodicals.

Concepts for Writing

You are beginning a journey into the intricacies of a kind of writing different from what you've known before—researched writing. You will experience many activities that go beyond typical middle and high school writing assignments, but you will be using all the strategies and elements of these previous writings. Researched writing builds on what you have already learned and adds to it. However, elements of researched writing go together in a different way.

Part of this new approach includes using other people's thoughts and conclusions. To their thoughts and conclusions you will add your own; otherwise, you will merely be making a report of what others have said. You will learn to evaluate what others have said about a particular subject and decide if what they have said actually fits with what you are trying to find out. You will learn how to distinguish the validity and trustworthiness of what you read. You will come to appreciate the difference between *good* writing and mediocre or poor writing. You will become very familiar with one or even several libraries and learn what they have to offer you the consumer, the academician, and the future tax payer. You will become familiar with the art of interviewing: learning through organized question-and-answer conversation what other people know that might be useful to your point of interest. In order to build a common language for communication, you will define terminology that is universal to a research community.

Hopefully, throughout the activities planned for each lesson in this research guide, you will see the necessity of developing researched writing skills that surpass typical skills used in essay writing. You will conclude that researched writing is useful in day-to-day life whether you are involved in business, academic, home, or church ventures because your writing skills will improve. Two major criteria for understanding the benefits of writing research include your attitude and your willingness.

Concepts for
Thinking

Thinking skills usually develop from the concrete to the more complex as you mature, developing mentally and physically. The more complex your thinking becomes, the more able you are to participate in such activities as understanding, applying, analyzing, evaluating, and creating. Scholars call these acts of thinking the *cognitive process dimension*. Thinking skills follow four major kinds of *knowledge dimensions*: factual knowledge, conceptual knowledge, procedural knowledge, and metacognitive knowledge. Because the skills used in researching and writing necessitate the use of all these dimensions of knowledge, scholars consider writing research an exercise in *higher-level thinking*—going far beyond the concrete thinking small children use when they learn that a furry animal that has four legs and barks is called a dog.

Writing research requires that you live with a subject or topic for several weeks as you explore it in more ways than you can even imagine now. For that reason, carefully choosing your topic or subject is of prime importance. You want to research something that you are truly invested in. If not, you will more likely lose interest, and the journey will lose its intrigue. Sometimes educators assign a topic to you, and you have no choice other than to adapt your attitude and determine to learn something new about something you might not otherwise consider. However, choosing your own research topic can sometimes be even harder because you can't really think of anything particular you want to research. The point is to choose carefully and definitely not hastily—you will be living with this subject for many weeks.

Higher-Level
Thinking Skills:
*Knowledge
Dimensions*
(Anderson 26-31)

Factual **Knowledge:** the basic elements to become acquainted with a subject or to solve a problem; terminology, specific details, and elements.

Example: You want to make pancakes for breakfast. You know you need ingredients, something to mix the ingredients in, some source of heat, and information about how long to cook them. This information is *concrete factual* knowledge.

Conceptual **Knowledge:** interrelationships among basic elements within a larger structure that enable them to function together; classifications and categories, principles and generalizations, theories, models, and structures.

Example: For making pancakes you need instructions about putting ingredients together to accomplish your desired outcome—pancakes; understanding that, you need both dry ingredients and liquid ingredients; you understand that certain amounts of these ingredients are necessary to result in a pancake rather than soup. This information is *conceptual* knowledge.

Procedural **Knowledge:** how to do something; methods of inquiry; criteria for using skills, techniques, and methods; subject-specific skills, subject specific techniques and methods; criteria for determining when to use appropriate procedures.

    Example: For making pancakes you need to know how to operate the stove, how to measure ingredients, how to combine ingredients, which cooking utensils to use, how to time the cooking process, which cooking procedure to use (if you boil the batter, you no longer have a *pancake!*). This information is *procedural* knowledge.

Metacognitive **Knowledge:** knowledge of cognition in general as well as awareness and knowledge of one's own cognition; strategic knowledge; knowledge about cognitive tasks, including appropriate contextual and conditional knowledge; self-knowledge.

    Example: You decide to make pancakes and follow through with the process, enjoy the pancakes for breakfast, and realize that following directions and having basic kitchen skills allows you to cook for yourself and even teach someone else how. You experience a certain amount of satisfaction that you can care for yourself. This information is *metacognitive* knowledge.

Factual Knowledge: terminology, details, elements

Conceptual Knowledge: interrelationships among basic elements

Procedural Knowledge: subject specific skills, techniques, methods, criteria

Metacognitive Knowledge: knowledge of general cognition; awareness and knowledge of own cognition: strategic knowledge, cognitive tasks, contextual and conditional knowledge; self-knowledge

**Summary:
Knowledge
Dimensions**

Higher-Level Thinking Skills:
Cognitive Process Dimensions
(Anderson 26-31)

Within each of these levels of knowledge dimensions, there are several layers of thinking (cognitive) processes:

Remember (recognizing, recalling): retrieve relevant knowledge from long-term memory

Understand (interpreting, exemplifying, classifying, summarizing, inferring, comparing, explaining): construct meaning from instructional messages, including oral, written, and graphic communication

Apply (executing, implementing): carry out or use a procedure in a given situation

Analyze (differentiating, organizing, attributing): break material into its constituent parts and determine how the parts relate to one another and to an overall structure or purpose

Evaluate (checking, critiquing): make judgments based on criteria and standards

Create (generating, planning, producing): put elements together to form a coherent or functional whole; reorganize elements into a new pattern or structure

Each knowledge and cognitive dimension builds on the others and is incorporated within the next higher level. Processing through these levels enables you to think in more developed ways. The obvious goal is to be able to think metacognitively on the highest creative level. Thinking **metacognitively** on the **creative** level means you are demonstrating the capability to think factually, conceptually, and procedurally through remembering, understanding, applying, analyzing, and evaluating. *Writing research is an excellent means of cultivating the highest level thinking skills inherent in all these knowledge and cognitive dimensions.*

INTRODUCING
*WRITING
RESEARCH
PAPERS*

Each week's activities in this research guide direct you through particular strategies that ultimately lead you to a finished piece of researched writing— *student published research.*

Each week you will see ASSIGNMENTS that notify you of the week's expectations and how to accomplish them. You and your educator will participate in EVALUATION FORMS that check weekly on your progress throughout the researched writing process. These weekly evaluations are a significant portion of your final Research Project evaluation. Following the research assignments, you will see **SAT Preparation Prompts** and **SAT Essay Writing Prompts** that aid your study for the SAT college entrance test, as well as refine your writing techniques for accomplishing this and all other writing projects.

Now that you know a bit about research and its strategies and how it can benefit you and society, let's move on . . . .

In this first week of assignments, remember you set the scene for the rest of the study. You organize your materials and learn what is expected of you.

1. Preparation for research: Read all the information in this lesson to begin learning the basics of researched writing.

Preparation for Research

2. Research Portfolio: Organize and label a three-ringed binder, preferably with pockets in the front and back; you need 5 major divisions labeled Interviews, Research Language, Evaluations, Essays, and Research Project. (See Appendix G)

Research Portfolio

3. Research language: Define the following terms using this lesson, the Appendix, and a dictionary if necessary: *knowledge dimensions, cognitive process dimensions, on-line, card catalogue, Dewey Decimal System, Library of Congress System, computerized catalog, electronic databases, CD-ROM, research, communication, style, essay, library, reference, source, write.*

Research Language

Since you are learning research language, file these terms, labeled and dated, in the Research Language section of your Research Portfolio for continued reference.

Higher-level thinking: Review the information presented in this lesson about knowledge and cognitive process dimensions of higher-level thinking skills. Remember that writing research is an excellent means of cultivating the highest level thinking because you incorporate all these dimensions during the process of researching and writing.

Collaborative Learning Interview

4. Collaborative learning interview with a professional librarian. Enter into a collaborative learning experience by arranging for an interview with a professional librarian; plan questions for the interview; take notes during the interview; organize the notes.

Step A: Call your local library and/or as many college or university libraries as is practical and inquire about a library tour and a twenty to thirty minute interview. Plan to tour at least two libraries and to interview two librarians. Courteously state your reasons for requesting the tour and interview: you are about to enter into a research project that requires knowledge of the library and the use of its facilities, and you need the guidance of an expert.

Step B: Plan what you need to know regarding access to the library:

1. services the library provides

2. location of books, including reference books

3. location of periodicals and microfiche

4. computer accessibility and programs

5. map of the library

Step C: Write your questions, leaving enough space after each question to take notes on what the librarian explains to you.

Step D: Organize the results of your tour and interview into a form that will aid your memory for the next visit.

Evaluations

5. Evaluations: Through evaluation you identify what you already know, what you don't know at all, and what you need to learn. Making these distinctions is part of the metacognitive knowledge dimension—higher-level thinking. Realizing what you don't know is one of the prerequisites for learning. After this week of preparing to explore researching and writing, you will have a better idea about what you need to learn.

A. Both you and your teacher should independently complete a
RESEARCH EVALUATION FORM and an ESSAY EVALUATION
FORM; yours is located at the end of this lesson; the teacher's is located in
the teacher edition of this book.

B. Compare the forms to gain perspective about your experience with this
part of the research learning process and with the writing process.

C. Insert the forms into the **Evaluations Section** of your Research Portfolio. Each week you will be evaluating yourself with two different evaluation forms: the research process and the SAT preparation components
(Grammar, diction, and usage; Essay Writing).

RESEARCH EVALUATION FORM: STUDENT

Lesson One

Student _____

Date _____

Evaluator _____

Concepts: introducing *Writing Research Papers*

	Possible Points	*Earned Points*
Readings of background and concepts completed	(20 points)	_____
Research portfolio organized and labeled	(10 points)	_____
Research language defined	(10 points)	_____
Library toured	(20 points)	_____
Interview completed	(20 points)	_____
Student evaluation completed	(10 points)	_____
Teacher evaluation completed	(10 points)	_____

If you don't fully understand the concepts in this lesson, please review them before you move to the next step.

Student's Self-Score for *Lesson One* _____

6. SAT Preparation Prompts

The following SAT section will help prepare you for the Scholastic Aptitude Test, a standard college entrance exam. In 2005 the SAT was revised to include additional requirements in the English field. Completing these sections in each lesson will help prepare you for this test and will also enhance your thinking and writing skills. According to *The Official SAT Study Guide for the New SAT* (99), there are three types of multiple-choice questions: identifying sentence errors, improving sentences, and improving paragraphs. Forty-nine questions on grammar and usage test your ability to use language in a consistently clear manner and to improve writing by the use of revision and editing. The multiple-choice questions don't ask you to define or use grammatical terms and don't test spelling or capitalization. Punctuation helps you know the correct answer. Because of these additions to the SAT, this curriculum includes practice with identifying sentence errors and improving sentences.

Grammar, diction, and usage equals two-thirds of your writing score on the SAT. The essay portion equals the other one-third.

The sentences in this section may contain errors in grammar, usage, choice of words, or idioms. Either there is just one error in a sentence or the sentence is correct. Some words or phrases are underlined and lettered; everything else in the sentence is correct.

**Grammar, Diction,
and Usage:
Identifying
Sentence Errors**

If an underlined word or phrase is incorrect, choose that letter; if the sentence is correct, select **No error**. Then blacken the appropriate space.

1. According to several of the <u>children, Mr. Macklin</u> has stated <u>that he expects </u>his children to
                                       A   B

provide care <u>for he and his wife,</u> which is one barrier <u>towards his considering</u> a different
                   C   D

discharge plan. <u>No error.</u>
                E

(A)   (B)   (C)   (D)   (E)

2. <u>Both England and Spain</u> shared in literary <u>efforts resulting</u> in the concepts of chivalry and
           A   B

honor that developed from a common source, <u>spreading throughout the world</u>, <u>suffered a decline</u>,
                                                           C   D

and ultimately revived through the pens of great scholars. <u>No error.</u>
                                               E

(A)   (B)   (C)   (D)   (E)

3. <u>While Madame Defarge's stifled self</u> stalks <u>revenge and Darnay's</u> seeks <u>family security Dickens'</u>
              A   B   C

repressed soul <u>keeps</u> a constant vigil searching for a suitable maternal figure. <u>No error.</u>
         D   E

(A)   (B)   (C)   (D)   (E)

4. The children have also <u>mentioned that while</u> Jan has admitted <u>that her and her husband</u> are no
                                   A   B

longer safe <u>at home, she is</u> unwilling to go against her husband's <u>wishes and will</u> abide by
                   C   D

whatever he says. <u>No error.</u>
                 E

(A)   (B)   (C)   (D)   (E)

7. SAT Essay Writing

The SAT "assesses your ability to develop and express ideas effectively; [it] evaluate[s] your ability to do the kind of writing required in college—writing that develops a point of view, presents ideas logically and clearly, and uses precise language . . . [the essay is] written in a limited time, which doesn't allow for many revisions, so it is considered and scored as a first draft" (Official 99).

Use this curriculum to prepare for the revised edition of the SAT, which includes writing and grammar elements in addition to three critical reading sections. Use the following pages dedicated to essay writing; they will help you organize and write your thoughts into essay format. Evaluation forms follow: one for you, and one for the sample SAT essay.

Successful writing includes:

1. A clearly expressed thesis statement

2. Well-developed ideas with relevant and accurate supporting information

3. Good organization

4. Appropriate, accurate, and varied vocabulary

5. Variety of sentence structure (syntax)

(Official 106)

The SAT allows you 46 lines on which to write between 300 and 400 words in a persuasive essay. It is important to write legibly because graders will spend approximately one to two minutes reading your essay. They will not spend time trying to decipher your handwriting. Use your two pages wisely, not writing in large letters or leaving extra wide margins. Your goal is to persuade your reader of your position.

Planning Essay One

Allot three to five minutes to think about and plan the essay—choosing between contrasting statements. Understand the statement and take a position.

Write about the following statement in two pages; you have *no more than twenty-five minutes.*

Respond to the statement:

Librarians hold the key to volumes of knowledge.

Assignment: The statement above implies that librarians have the power to unlock the secrets of knowledge contained in libraries. Do you agree or disagree? Write a persuasive essay supporting, disputing, or qualifying the statement. You may use examples from history, literature, popular culture, current events, or personal experience to support your position.

Initial thoughts about this statement:

_____

_____

Do I agree or disagree with this statement?

_____

_____

Reasons/support/evidence for my position (why I maintain this position):

I. Example from history, literature, popular culture, current events, or personal experience:

_____

_____

II. Example from history, literature, popular culture, current events, or personal experience:

_____

_____

III. Example from history, literature, popular culture, current events, or personal experience:

_____

_____

These thoughts become the outline for your essay. Do not take more than three to five minutes to organize these thoughts. These first *three to five minutes are crucial to the thinking skills* you will exhibit in the essay.

You will need *the next twenty minutes to persuade your audience* of your position on the issue, to support your position as you move from idea to idea, and to use appropriate vocabulary and varied sentence structure free from grammar, mechanics, and usage errors.

It is important not to change your position in the middle of the essay because you won't have time to rework the essay.

You are now ready to write the essay on two sheets of paper. Your goal is to write between 300 and 400 words on the issue.

It is very important to *time the writing*.

Librarians Hold the Key
Essay One

Your Title:

_____

_____

_____

_____

_____

_____

_____

_____

_____

_____

_____

_____

_____

_____

_____

_____

_____

_____

_____

Practice Essay Evaluation Form: Student

Lesson One

Evaluate your essay using the following criteria as a guide; a scoring section follows this chart.

Level 6	Level 5	Level 4	Level 3	Level 2	Level 1
Insightful - Outstanding	**Effective - Solid**	**Competent - Adequate**	**Inadequate - Limited**	**Seriously flawed**	**Deficient**
Convincing development of a position on the issue	Proficient, coherent development of a position on the issue	Workmanlike development of a position on the issue	Sketchy development of a position on the issue	Limited development of a position on the issue	Lack of a position on the issue
Selection of relevant examples and evidence to support writer's position	Selection of basically relevant evidence to support writer's position	Selection of reasonably appropriate evidence to support writer's position	Selection of weak or inappropriate evidence to support writer's position	Selection of weak or inappropriate evidence to support writer's position	Absence of evidence to support a point of view
Smooth, well-orchestrated progression from idea to idea	Relatively well-ordered progression from idea to idea	Acceptable progression from idea to idea	Erratic progression from idea to idea	Tendency toward incoherence	Absence of focus and organization
Use of varied sentence types and appropriate vocabulary	Reasonably varied sentence structure and reasonable vocabulary	Somewhat varied sentence structure and somewhat varied vocabulary	Somewhat limited vocabulary and inadequately varied sentence structure	Highly limited vocabulary and numerous problems with sentence structure	Rudimentary vocabulary and severe problems with sentence structure
Freedom from most technical flaws (grammar, usage, diction)	Relative freedom from technical flaws	Some flaws in mechanics, usage, and grammar	Multiple flaws in mechanics, usage, and grammar	Errors in mechanics, usage, and grammar serious enough to interfere with the reader's comprehension	Extensive flaws in mechanics, usage, and grammar severe enough to block the reader's comprehension

(Barron's 301, Kaplan 21, Official 105)

Level 6: demonstrates a clear command of writing and thinking skills despite the occasional, infrequent minor error.

Level 5: exhibits a generally dependable command of writing and thinking skills despite some mistakes.

Level 4: exhibits a generally adequate command of writing and thinking skills although the skills are typically inconsistent in quality.

Level 3: exhibits an insufficient command of writing and thinking skills although the skills show some signs of developing proficiency.

Level 2: exhibits a quite flawed command of writing and thinking skills.

Level 1: exhibits an acutely flawed command of writing and thinking skills.

Student's self-score of essay (between 1 and 6) _____

Read the following essay and then determine the score you would give it based on the scoring criteria and word count. Note inconsistencies in thinking.

Sample Student Essay

Respond to the statement:

"If you would keep your secret from an enemy, tell it not to a friend."

—Ben Franklin

<u>Assignment:</u> The statement above implies that friends are not responsible to keep secrets. Write an essay supporting, disputing, or qualifying the statement. You may use examples from history, literature, popular culture, current events, or personal experience to support your position.

Don't Tell Anybody

If you have something you don't want anybody else to know then you'd better not tell it to anybody. People and relationships change all the time and sometimes you count some people as your friends today but then they turn on you and become your enemies tomorrow. They could easily hurt you and you probable wouldn't want to be around them anymore. If that happens, whatever you tell them while they were your "friends" will remain with them even after they became your "enemies." Therefore your secrets guarded from the ones you didn't like would then belong to them those people switched relationships. Also, people in general have a hole lot of problem keeping their mouths shut regarding nice juicy pieces of gossip. If you tell your friend some good old gossip about somebody else you can be real sure that it will circle around a hole bunch of people and reach the person you wanted to hide the information from. To be safe, resist the temptation to gabble a whole lot about other peoples business remains a sure-fire approach to steering clear of gossip mixups. Ben Franklin's remark is pretty sad because if it refers to a person confiding a secret in someone he considers a true friend. That friend considered so trustworthy may very well back-stab him by breaking the trust and spilling the secret to anyone. It is a sobering fact about humans often our pledged loyalties are fragel and forgotten when a better chance comes along. Oh, well. You just do what you can, put a little trust in a few people you think you have a little bit of safety with and slowly risk exposing your heart to them. Sometimes your going to be mocked and sometimes accepted with some respect. Its just the way life is. _____

_____

_____

_____

_____

_____

_____

_____

_____

_____

_____

_____

Evaluate the student's essay using the following criteria as a guide; a scoring section follows this chart.

SAMPLE ESSAY EVALUATION FORM

Lesson One

Level 6	Level 5	Level 4	Level 3	Level 2	Level 1
Insightful - Outstanding	Effective - Solid	Competent - Adequate	Inadequate - Limited	Seriously flawed	Deficient
Convincing development of a position on the issue	Proficient, coherent development of a position on the issue	Workmanlike development of a position on the issue	Sketchy development of a position on the issue	Limited development of a position on the issue	Lack of a position on the issue
Selection of relevant examples and evidence to support writer's position	Selection of basically relevant evidence to support writer's position	Selection of reasonably appropriate evidence to support writer's position	Selection of weak or inappropriate evidence to support writer's position	Selection of weak or inappropriate evidence to support writer's position	Absence of evidence to support a point of view
Smooth, well-orchestrated progression from idea to idea	Relatively well-ordered progression from idea to idea	Acceptable progression from idea to idea	Erratic progression from idea to idea	Tendency toward incoherence	Absence of focus and organization
Use of varied sentence types and appropriate vocabulary	Reasonably varied sentence structure and reasonable vocabulary	Somewhat varied sentence structure and somewhat varied vocabulary	Somewhat limited vocabulary and inadequately varied sentence structure	Highly limited vocabulary and numerous problems with sentence structure	Rudimentary vocabulary and severe problems with sentence structure
Freedom from most technical flaws (grammar, usage, diction)	Relative freedom from technical flaws	Some flaws in mechanics, usage, and grammar	Multiple flaws in mechanics, usage, and grammar	Errors in mechanics, usage, and grammar serious enough to interfere with the reader's comprehension	Extensive flaws in mechanics, usage, and grammar severe enough to block the reader's comprehension

(Barron's 301, Kaplan 21, Official 105)
Level 6: demonstrates a clear command of writing and thinking skills despite the occasional, infrequent minor error.
Level 5: exhibits a generally dependable command of writing and thinking skills despite some mistakes.
Level 4: exhibits a generally adequate command of writing and thinking skills although the skills are typically inconsistent in quality.
Level 3: exhibits an insufficient command of writing and thinking skills although the skills show some signs of developing proficiency.
Level 2: exhibits a quite flawed command of writing and thinking skills.
Level 1: exhibits an acutely flawed command of writing and thinking skills.

Student's self-score of essay (between 1 and 6) _____
[Based on the criteria and considering the length of the essay, the evaluator's score for this essay is 2.
The student was unable to meet the assignment length and has many errors and inconsistencies.]

Sample Student Essay

Read the following essay and then determine the score you would give it based on the scoring criteria and word count. This student's essay is around 400 words.

Respond to the statement:

The field of humanities equips individuals for life.

Assignment: The statement above implies that the field of humanities is an important part of life's experiences. Write an essay supporting, disputing, or qualifying the statement. You may use examples from history, literature, popular culture, current events, or personal experience to support your position.

Life-Equipping Humanities

"Humanities" is a broad term for the varying aspects of the human life and how these eclectic dimensions relate to one another. Such facets as language, literature, philosophy, history, religion, psychology, and mythology all pinpoint specific areas of a person's world and somehow meld together to produce a multi-faceted and multi-talented individual. Though I have lived only sixteen years, I feel that I own fairly tested experiences with the relationships between the many elements of life. The last quarter of my freshman year I lived apart from my family on a ranch in Montana. With 75 other teenagers I went to school, took special interests classes, attended and helped lead several teen-issue centered groups, and learned innumerable lessons of life. My everyday circles in my home town consist mainly of white, middle class, educated families; in Montana I experienced a very different environment. I observed, interacted with and learned from Native Americans, Mexicans, immigrants, African-Americans and Caucasians of all different social and economic classes, from all different backgrounds, and with all different perspectives on and experiences in life. Throughout my time in Montana, I took in many other people's angles of life and discovered and deepened my worldview.

Language arts have been instilled firmly in me from my childhood. My mother, an English teacher, has constantly opened my mind to the power of words through reading to me at night as a child and encouraging me to probe my world through journaling my thoughts and experiences. I have kept detailed journals for as long as I can remember, filling them with my responses to the days' events, stories and poems. I have several older siblings, all of whom are either in college or are/have been working on post-graduate degrees. Because of their desire to communicate their learning, I was exposed early to educational and philosophical issues. Many conversations about history and its relation to the present and future have sparked my mind to explore my heritage and the world before me. I am acquainted with several mental health workers and have participated in discussions of psychology, asking and learning about the often unspoken parts of people. These many experiences have molded my views of life and of myself. I am extremely interested in gaining further experiences that enable me to learn from and offer to others glimpses of understanding the world. _____

_____

_____

_____

_____

_____

SAMPLE ESSAY
EVALUATION
FORM

Lesson One

Evaluate the student's essay using the following criteria as a guide; a scoring section follows this chart.

Level 6	Level 5	Level 4	Level 3	Level 2	Level 1
Insightful - Outstanding	Effective - Solid	Competent - Adequate	Inadequate - Limited	Seriously flawed	Deficient
Convincing development of a position on the issue	Proficient, coherent development of a position on the issue	Workmanlike development of a position on the issue	Sketchy development of a position on the issue	Limited development of a position on the issue	Lack of a position on the issue
Selection of relevant examples and evidence to support writer's position	Selection of basically relevant evidence to support writer's position	Selection of reasonably appropriate evidence to support writer's position	Selection of weak or inappropriate evidence to support writer's position	Selection of weak or inappropriate evidence to support writer's position	Absence of evidence to support a point of view
Smooth, well-orchestrated progression from idea to idea	Relatively well-ordered progression from idea to idea	Acceptable progression from idea to idea	Erratic progression from idea to idea	Tendency toward incoherence	Absence of focus and organization
Use of varied sentence types and appropriate vocabulary	Reasonably varied sentence structure and reasonable vocabulary	Somewhat varied sentence structure and somewhat varied vocabulary	Somewhat limited vocabulary and inadequately varied sentence structure	Highly limited vocabulary and numerous problems with sentence structure	Rudimentary vocabulary and severe problems with sentence structure
Freedom from most technical flaws (grammar, usage, diction)	Relative freedom from technical flaws	Some flaws in mechanics, usage, and grammar	Multiple flaws in mechanics, usage, and grammar	Errors in mechanics, usage, and grammar serious enough to interfere with the reader's comprehension	Extensive flaws in mechanics, usage, and grammar severe enough to block the reader's comprehension

(Barron's 301, Kaplan 21, Official 105)

Level 6: demonstrates a clear command of writing and thinking skills despite the occasional, infrequent minor error.
Level 5: exhibits a generally dependable command of writing and thinking skills despite some mistakes.
Level 4: exhibits a generally adequate command of writing and thinking skills although the skills are typically inconsistent in quality.
Level 3: exhibits an insufficient command of writing and thinking skills although the skills show some signs of developing proficiency.
Level 2: exhibits a quite flawed command of writing and thinking skills.
Level 1: exhibits an acutely flawed command of writing and thinking skills.

Student's self-score of sample essay (between 1 and 6) _____
[Using the criteria and considering the assigned length of the essay, the SAT evaluator's score for this essay is 5].

LESSON TWO

INITIATING WRITING RESEARCH

A. Concepts

**Lesson Two
Overview**

1. Timeline and deadlines

2. Library and computer familiarity

3. Developing a working bibliography

4. Choosing the subject or research question

5. Formulating a thesis statement

6. Audience

B. Assignments

1. Collaborative learning interview: friend or family researcher

2. Research language: *thesis, audience, bibliography, working bibliography, hypothesis, enthymeme, periodical, Works Cited, style manuals*

3. Research portfolio

4. Evaluations

5. SAT prep prompts: grammar, diction, and usage—identifying sentence errors; essay writing

6. Sample essay

CONCEPTS

INITIATING
WRITING
RESEARCH

**Timeline
and
Deadline**

By now you have had discussions with your educator, and the two of you have decided on a timeline for your research. You know whether you chose the four-week plan or the eight-week plan, when you started, and when you expect to finish. You made these decisions based on your academic work load, your past experience with research, your level of writing skill, and the time available for researching and writing. Since you know the beginning and the end of the timeline, the next logical step is to determine how much needs to be accomplished each week, and then each day, in order to get the project completed on time. That's where this weekly plan is helpful. If you work through all the assignments every week, you will meet your goal. Having a workable plan greatly reduces the stress with any project. A really good way to plan your eight weeks of researching and writing is to have a calendar of activities at your main workplace (See Appendix A or B). As you finish each assignment, put a check in the day's block and enjoy the feeling of accomplishment as your project grows.

**Library and
Computer
Familiarity**

Since you have visited the library, interviewed a professional librarian, taken a tour, and been informed about library resources (including computer tools and programs), you also have a general idea of where to find different kinds of books, references books, periodicals, microfiche, maps, or other library resources. You have given thought to the available resources because that will partially determine the type of research you do. If you have access to a university or college library, your resources are more extensive than if you are restricted to a local neighborhood library. Computers can open entire libraries to you if you have the proper programs and accessibility. Whatever your available resources, learn to use the library and the computer to their maximum capacity. For many educators, using only the Internet for research is *not* an acceptable research strategy, particularly for those new to research. Computers are exceptionally useful, but discerning between reliable and non-reliable information requires extreme proficiency.

Learning the availability of sources and resources is invaluable for choosing your topic of inquiry. Keep that in mind as you identify exactly what you want to research.

**Working
Bibliography**

A working bibliography will contain works that have been read for general knowledge but may not actually be used in the Works Cited pages. A working bibliography is an organized listing of books, periodicals, pamphlets, interviews, news broadcasts, speakers, Internet or *any reference* that informs your research. For our purposes, the working bibliography is a set of 3x5 index cards with source material on it. These are known as bibliography cards.

All sources (places you get information) that you actually use must be noted as the Works Cited at the end of your research paper. The references to the works (the notes that you use—called footnotes or endnotes or internal notes) and the source material must coordinate. For instance, if you quote from David Dark's *The Gospel According to America*, you will follow a standard pattern that assures your audience that you got this direct quotation from that author's book. You will include the author's name, the title of the book, the publication information, and the page numbers from which you got the information.

The methods for recording these patterns are very specific, and they vary according to style manuals and whether the information came from a book, a periodical (scholarly journal, magazine, or newspaper), or even an interview. (See the following note about various style manuals). That way, if your readers decide to read more about this information, they will have the information they need to find your quotation in the book. In your finished research project you will not include bibliographical entries than you have not used for quotations, summaries, or paraphrases. Conversely, you *will* have at least one note card and one Works Cited entry for every quotation, summary, or paraphrase you used in your research project. Not doing so results in plagiarism.

For the purposes of learning research and gaining experience with strategies and formatting, include the following types of sources in your *working bibliography*:

6-8 books (including references books)

5-6 periodicals (any combination of scholarly journals, magazines, newspapers; these sources may give you more recent information about your topic than books)

1-2 microforms (microfilm, microfiche)

1-2 reliable and valid Internet sources

For the Works Cited at the conclusion of your project, include at least

4-5 books (including references books)

3-4 periodicals (any combination of scholarly journals, magazines, newspapers)

1-2 microforms (microfilm, microfiche)

1-2 reliable and valid Internet sources

Typically, if you are researching in the humanities field (language and literature), you will use the MLA Style Manual. If you are researching in the social sciences field (psychology, education), you will use the APA Style Manual. If you are researching in the field of religion, you will use the Turabian (or *Chicago Manual of Style*). Of course, your school, educator, or business may choose which style is preferred, and you will follow that guideline.

To perfect the formatting for note taking and bibliography cards, consult a thorough grammar handbook. (Also, see Lessons Five and Six and Appendices E and H.) A sample bibliography card is provided below, but it is just that—a sample from the *many* variations. Do not use this sample as your *only* pattern for every bibliographical entry in your research paper.

Sample Bibliography Card

Since this card is bibliographical, it will not have notes on it. This card represents the place where you will find the information that is quoted, summarized, or paraphrased on its coordinating 4x6 note card. Both the note card and the bibliography card pertain to **Major Heading I Sub-Heading A**. Note that this particular source is an edited book that does not have a specific author.

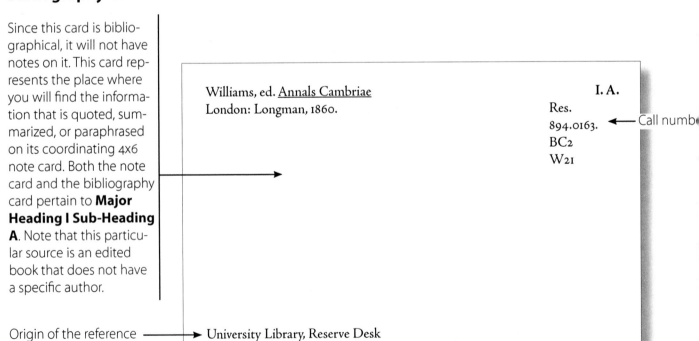

Williams, ed. Annals Cambriae
London: Longman, 1860.

I. A.
Res.
894.0163. ← Call numbe
BC2
W21

Origin of the reference → University Library, Reserve Desk

When you are ready to convert the sources from your working bibliography into the Works Cited, you will get the information from these bibliography cards. Properly formatting them now lessens your work later.

Choosing the Topic or Subject

Often, a major difficulty for students is determining what to research. Sometimes that quandary is decided for you if the teacher provides the topic or question. For instance, if you are researching for a literature class, your educator may want you to learn more about a particular author or a particular piece of fiction, poetry, or drama. If you are writing research for a history class, your educator may want you to learn more about a president's reform policy or a specific historical era. Research for a math class may center on the evolution of calculators from slide rules. Being provided the subject or topic may simplify the initial stages of the research, but it may also limit you if you really have interest in another topic. What happens, however, if the educator's goal is the actual research process, and the topic or question is left up to you? What happens if you have no idea what to research? How do you know where to begin? How do you limit or expand a subject or question after you have begun?

First, think about what you really enjoy. What do you like to do in your free time? What do you love to read? What do you wish you had some way of knowing? Is there a place you'd like to visit? A person you'd like to know more about? A concept you've heard about but don't understand? Something you've always wondered? Are there *two things* you really like but are having difficulty choosing between? Reflecting on your interests is an excellent way to investigate potential subjects, topics, or questions.

Suppose you love music, playing the guitar is a favorite pastime, and you've always wondered why that round hole is in the guitar. What would happen if the hole were square or rectangular? Who decided that the hole should be round in the guitar? Why does the sound differ depending on how you pluck the string? Have guitars always looked like they do today? What is the best kind of wood for making a guitar? By doing a little mental exploration, you can devise numerous questions about something that interests you greatly; you can have a research topic that evolves into or from a question. Then, you're on your way.

As you read books and magazines and scholarly journals, you'll begin to see different kinds of information about your question, and you'll begin to learn about the availability of the information—is there a great deal of information or only a little? This part of scan-reading and purposeful wandering around the library is the initial stage of determining your research topic or question and whether or not you find far too much information or not nearly enough to continue the search. If it's far too much, you'll need to narrow the focus of your subject; if there's very little information, you'll need to expand the focus of your subject. For instance, if you are trying to answer the research question, "*Who discovered that the hole in the guitar should be round?*" and you find only one source that mentions anything about the "who," you'll need to alter your question to something like, "*Why is the hole in the guitar round?*" Later, you might be able to include the *who* within the discovery about the *why* for the guitar's hole.

Computer databases can be very helpful in this initial phase of research. Ask your librarian for help. Use an Internet keyword search to find sites quickly. Use the library's database to find and narrow a subject. Some databases include InfoTrac, PsycINFO, ERIC, Health & Wellness (Lester 23).

**Wider
Thinking**

When trying to decide between two very interesting and important bodies of information, it is sometimes possible to blend them into one research project. In other words, if you are taking European History and the teacher requires a research paper, you might be able to write it to also satisfy the requirements for a World Literature English course. Another example: Suppose you are taking Spanish and English in the same academic year. To satisfy the research requirement in English you'd like to find some way to combine these two subjects in one writing project. You will need to find a common ground between the two fields of study. You might ask yourself what English and Spanish Literatures have in common, if anything. If you already know that in English Literature, Britain had her King Arthur and his chivalry, you have a beginning point.

Also, if you've already studied enough Spanish to know that the concept of pundanor (honor, pride) is prominent in Spanish literature, you have a possible connection. The question might be, "Is there any evidence that King Arthur's chivalry in England had anything to do with Spanish pundanor?" You would need to investigate both sets of literature to determine if English chivalry and Spanish pundanor have a commonality, and perhaps, how they came to have the harmony. These are very extensive branches of knowledge and far too wide-ranging for a beginning research paper, but they could be narrowed to a more manageable topic. The final thesis could look something like this: King Arthur's code of chivalry influenced the literature of Spain's Pedro Calderón de la Barca.

Formulating a Thesis Statement

After the initial reading and purposeful wandering in the library, you'll be ready to think about developing a thesis statement. It will probably change as you continue searching for information and as your interest develops—that's perfectly acceptable. You will probably word the statement/question one way and then another way several times before you finally decide what it is you are trying to discover. However, deciding fairly early in the research process is necessary, or you may wander around the library or the computer database, seeing more and more possibilities and varieties of information and getting more and more overwhelmed at the volumes of information. Generally, try to have your thesis determined by the time you start writing the first draft.

For planning purposes, consider looking for three or four strands of information about your topic/question. You may begin the research with the question, "Why is the hole in the guitar round?" and after considerable reading and researching, you discover that "The hole in the guitar is round because of X, Y, and Z." The first example is a research question; the second one is a research statement derived from a question. Ultimately, your question-statement will evolve to include three or four strands of information. More than that will greatly lengthen your research project, which is fine if you have the time and interest in the subject. For our purposes in this research guide and to limit the length of the research paper, we will use the two-to-three strands approach.

Therefore, for example, your thesis statement could say, "The hole in the guitar is round because of body resonance, sound waves, and aesthetics." Both you and your audience know from that statement that your research revolves around three major points—the guitar's body resonance, sound waves, and aesthetics—those three points and no others. You have determined those three points from your scanning and readings. Regardless of how many other interesting things you might read about the guitar, they will not be included in this particular research project. You will not mention all the songs that can be played on the guitar, the history of the guitar throughout the nations, the many people who have played guitars, or all the countries that have guitars displayed in museums. Your project is *only* going to tell your audience about why the guitar's hole is round—because of body resonance, because of sound waves, and because of aesthetics. By working through this process and making these decisions, you have now limited your thesis statement and you know the direction of your research project. You know what you are going to be writing about and what you are *not* going to be writing about.

Thesis, Enthymeme, and Hypothesis— Three Methods of Exploring a Topic

Now that you are familiar with the idea of writing research, consider the following thesis statement that pertains to this book about writing research.

Example 1:

Thesis: Students use higher-level thinking skills as they systematically <u>research</u>, <u>reflect</u>, and <u>write</u> about a subject.

This thesis advances a conclusion that the writer will defend, and it supplies a purpose. The writer will defend researching, reflecting, and writing as a means of developing higher-level thinking. To write this curriculum, *Writing Research Papers with Confidence*, the processes of <u>researching</u>, <u>reflecting</u>, and <u>writing</u> had to be undertaken. As you progress through the strategies in this course, you may reflect on the research process and the writing techniques behind this curriculum itself. It will serve as a guide for your research and will help you see the benefits and results of the strategies and efforts.

Now consider the question about why the hole in the guitar
is round.

Example 2:

Enthymeme: The hole in the guitar is round because of the guitar's body
shape, sound waves, and player comfort.

One thesis-like method of exploring a topic is an enthymeme, which is
a claim supported with a *because* clause (Lester 24). This enthymeme
contains the word *because*, which signals readers that the writer is going
to explain and defend why the guitar hole is round. The claim that the
hole is round is supported by the stated reasons that body shape, sound
waves, and player comfort are conditions of the round-hole shape, not
other shapes, in the guitar. The writer will need to address that other
shapes do not satisfy the same expectations for guitars with round holes.

Consider another approach.

Example 3:

Hypothesis: The sound from a guitar is determined by the size of the
round hole.

A hypothesis is a theory (not a fact) which must be proven in a
laboratory or field experience through careful observation and
examination. It requires proof to make its claim valid. Everything about
the round hole and the claim that it controls the sound emanating from
the guitar must be tested and proven. You can also have a hypothesis
about a piece of literature; in that case you examine the theory through
careful literary analysis.

Study the following thesis statements to get a glimpse of how some students have worded a thesis.

Example 4: Enthymeme

Because of Khubilai's integration of Mongolian expansion and Chinese domestic policy, the Yüan Dynasty flourished before its ultimate decline from overexpansion and the emperor's overindulgence.

Example 5: Thesis

In "I Will Put Chaos Into Fourteen Lines" and in sonnet sequences *Fatal Interview* and *Sonnets from an Ungrafted Tree*, Edna St. Vincent Millay boldly challenges the male-dominance hidden in the traditional sonnet form.

Example 6: Thesis

Dickens records his own life experiences through chronicling his characters' needs, the negligence or nourishment of these needs, and the characters' reactions to how these needs are considered.

Example 7: Thesis

Due to his historical, mythical, and legendary background, King Arthur provided the basis from which chivalry and honor emerged.

Think about the many ways you can word your thesis, enthymeme, or hypothesis as you decide what you want to accomplish with your research. Defining your audience will help you decide. For practical purposes, the term *thesis* is used throughout this curriculum.

Audience

Whenever you research and then write about it, you most likely write for someone else as well as yourself. As you refine the thesis statement, keep in mind your audience. You will want to clarify the *purpose* for your audience: are you going to *persuade* your reader to think or do something because of your position in the paper? Are you going to *argue* a particular point of view? Are you going to *describe* something for the audience? Are you going to *explain* something to the audience? *Persuading, arguing, describing,* or *explaining* determines how you present the information for your audience.

Whoever that is—whether it's your teacher, your parents, your pastor, your business partner, or the President of the United States—that person or those people make up your audience. Everything you write will be written with your audience in mind as you *persuade, argue, describe,* or *explain.* You will be thinking about your audience as you research, think, read, and write. You will constantly be asking yourself if you are still addressing that particular audience and if you are still *persuading, arguing, describing,* or *explaining.* For instance, if the President wants to know why the hole in a guitar is round, you will be thinking about your role as informant to the President. Your business partner might have a different set of expectations for wanting to know why the hole in the guitar is round—perhaps she wants to determine if there are financial advantages for eliminating the hole altogether. The President, on the other hand, is considering giving hundreds of guitars to disadvantaged children who need a very player-friendly musical instrument. Knowing that your business partner is interested in finances, you may choose to argue through the results of your research that leaving the hole in the guitar is most advantageous for the company. Knowing that the President is interested in providing guitars to disadvantaged children may cause you to persuade him through your research that the guitar is *not* the most user-friendly musical instrument for disadvantaged children—in which case you will want to offer another option to the President! Thus, the audience helps you determine the focus of the research, how you write, what you emphasize, and which information is important.

ASSIGNMENTS

INITIATING
WRITING
RESEARCH

**Preliminaries
to Writing
Research**

1. Preliminaries to writing research

A. **Read** all the information in this lesson.

B. **Spend several hours** in the library and on the Internet (continuing to consult with the librarian) looking for information for the particular topic you have chosen or been assigned. Having an inquisitive attitude will make your work more pleasant.

C. **Begin** a preliminary bibliography.

**Collaborative
Learning
Interview**

2. **Collaborative learning interview** with a friend or family researcher. Enter into a collaborative learning experience by arranging for an interview with an adult friend or family member; plan questions for the interview; take notes during the interview; organize the notes. The purpose of this interview is to hear the research experiences of another friend or family member.

Step A: Call or personally arrange for a twenty-to-thirty minute meeting with the adult family member. Courteously state your reasons for requesting the interview: you are researching and would like the adult's insight into the importance and relevance of research and writing.

Step B: Plan what you need to know, especially how research and/or writing is pertinent to the adult's life and work; interviewing a grandparent might bring an interesting perspective to this assignment. Ask about the adult's experience with research, the availability of library and computer services when your adult was doing or does research, and what type of research was or is being done.

Step C: Write your questions, leaving enough space after each question to take notes on what the adult tells you. Be respectful, sensitive, and courteous—some adults may have never done academic research and you may hear a very different perspective.

Step D: Organize your interview; if it is helpful for your research, use it.

3. Research language: Define the following terms using the information in this lesson, the Appendix, and a dictionary if necessary: *thesis, audience, bibliography, working bibliography, hypothesis, enthymeme, periodical, Works Cited, style manuals.* Add these terms, labeled and dated, to the Research Language section of your Research Portfolio.

Research Language

4. Research portfolio: Continue organizing and labeling your three-ringed binder with its 5 major divisions—Interviews, Research Language, Evaluations, Essays, and Research Project. (See Appendix G)

Research Portfolio

Higher-level thinking: Continue to think about the information presented in Lesson One about knowledge and cognitive dimensions of higher-level thinking skills. Writing research is an excellent means of cultivating the highest-level thinking because you incorporate all these cognitive dimensions during the process of researching and writing.

Higher-level Thinking

5. Evaluations: Through evaluation you identify what you already know, what you don't know at all, and what you need to learn. Making these distinctions is part of the metacognitive knowledge dimension—higher-level thinking. Realizing what you don't know is one of the prerequisites for learning.

Evaluations

> **A.** Both you and your teacher should independently complete a *Research Evaluation Form* and an *Essay Evaluation Form;* yours is located at the end of this lesson.
>
> **B.** Compare the forms to gain perspective about your experience with this part of the research learning process and with the writing process.
>
> **C.** Insert the forms into the Evaluations Section of your Research Portfolio.

RESEARCH EVALUATION FORM: STUDENT

Lesson Two

Student _____

Date _____

Evaluator _____

Concepts: initiating writing research

	Possible Points	Earned Points
Readings of concepts completed	(20 points)	_____
Research portfolio organized and labeled	(10 points)	_____
Library and computer research continuing	(20 points)	_____
Working bibliography begun	(20 points)	_____
Interview completed	(10 points)	_____
Thesis discussed	(10 points)	_____
Student evaluation completed	(5 points)	_____
Teacher evaluation completed	(5 points)	_____

If you don't fully understand the concepts in this lesson, review the material before you move to the next step.

Student's Self-Score for *Lesson Two* _____

6. SAT Preparation Prompts

**SAT Preparation
Prompts**

The following SAT section will help prepare you for the Scholastic Aptitude Test, a standard college entrance exam. In 2005 the SAT was revised to include additional requirements in the English field. Completing these sections in each lesson will help prepare you for this test and will also enhance your thinking and writing skills. According to *The Official SAT Study Guide for the New SAT* (99), there are three types of multiple-choice questions: identifying sentence errors, improving sentences, and improving paragraphs. Forty-nine questions on grammar and usage test your ability to use language in a consistently clear manner and to improve writing by the use of revision and editing. The multiple-choice questions don't ask you to define or use grammatical terms and don't test spelling or capitalization. Punctuation helps you know the correct answer. Because of these additions to the SAT, this curriculum includes practice with identifying sentence errors and improving sentences.

Grammar, diction, and usage equals two-thirds of your writing score on the SAT. The essay portion equals the other one-third.

The sentences in this section may contain errors in grammar, usage, choice of words, or idioms. Either there is just one error in a sentence or the sentence is correct. Some words or phrases are underlined and lettered; everything else in the sentence is correct.

**Grammar, Diction,
and Usage:
Identifying
Sentence Errors**

If an underlined word or phrase is incorrect, choose that letter; if the sentence is correct, select **No error**. Then blacken the appropriate space.

1. Mr. Macklin stated that he is completely independent and that he also provides care
　　　A　　　　　　　B　　　　　　　　　　　　C
for he and his wife. No error.
　　　D　　　　E

(A)　(B)　(C)　(D)　(E)

2. <u>King Arthur's</u> historical, mythical, and legendary background provided the <u>basis from which</u>
   A   B

chivalry and honor <u>emerged, the legends</u> originated through works of <u>sixteenth century England's</u>
        C   D

Edmund Spenser and seventeenth century Spain's Pedro Calderón de la Barca. <u>No error.</u>
                             E

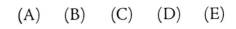

3. Darnay attempts to murder his <u>memories; they resurrect</u> when he returns to <u>France, though,</u>
              A   B

and <u>demand</u> a death in return <u>for his abandoning</u> them. <u>No error.</u>
  C   D   E

(A) (B) (C) (D) (E)

4. <u>While many families come</u> into therapy complaining about a specific <u>problem; structural</u>
      A   B

therapists want to look beyond <u>the individual problems</u> to the process <u>of family functioning.</u>
           C   D

<u>No error.</u>
 E
           (A) (B) (C) (D) (E)

7. SAT Essay Writing

The SAT "assesses your ability to develop and express ideas effectively; [it] evaluate[s] your ability to do the kind of writing required in college—writing that develops a point of view, presents ideas logically and clearly, and uses precise language . . . [the essay is] written in a limited time, which doesn't allow for many revisions, so it is considered and scored as a first draft" (Official 99).

Use this curriculum to prepare for the revised edition of the SAT, which includes writing and grammar elements in addition to three critical reading sections. Use the following pages dedicated to essay writing; they will help you organize and write your thoughts into essay format. Evaluation forms follow: one for you, and one for the sample SAT essay.

Successful writing includes:

1. A clearly expressed thesis statement

2. Well-developed ideas with relevant and accurate supporting information

3. Good organization

4. Appropriate, accurate, and varied vocabulary

5. Variety of sentence structure (syntax)

(Official 106)

The SAT allows you 46 lines on which to write between 300 and 400 words in a persuasive essay. It is important to write legibly because graders will spend approximately one to two minutes reading your essay. They will not spend time trying to decipher your handwriting. Use your two pages wisely, not writing in large letters or leaving extra wide margins. Your goal is to persuade your reader of your position.

Allot three to five minutes to think about and plan the essay—choosing between contrasting statements. Understand the statement and take a position.

**Planning Essay
Two**

Write about the following statement in two pages; you have *no more than twenty-five minutes.*

Choose between contrasting statements:

> *Researching unfamiliar knowledge broadens the mind's perspectives.*
> *Being content with what you already know solidifies perspective.*

Assignment: Consider the statements above. Choose the one that best represents your beliefs, and write an essay explaining your position. You may use examples from history, literature, popular culture, current events, or personal experience to support your position.

Initial thoughts about this statement:

_____

_____

Do I agree or disagree with this statement?

_____

_____

Reasons/support/evidence for my position (why I maintain this position):

I. Example from history, literature, popular culture, current events, or personal experience:

_____

_____

II. Example from history, literature, popular culture, current events, or personal experience:

_____

_____

III. Example from history, literature, popular culture, current events, or personal experience:

_____

_____

These thoughts become the outline for your essay. Do not take more than three to five minutes to organize these thoughts. These first *three to five minutes are crucial to the thinking skills* you will exhibit in the essay.

You will need the *next twenty minutes to persuade your audience* of your position on the issue, to support your position as you move from idea to idea, and to use appropriate vocabulary and varied sentence structure free from grammar, mechanics, and usage errors.

It is important not to change your position in the middle of the essay because you won't have time to rework the essay.

You are now ready to write the essay on two sheets of paper. Your goal is to write between 300 and 400 words on the issue.

It is very important to *time the writing*.

Perspectives on Knowledge
Essay Two

Your Title:

_____

_____

_____

_____

_____

_____

_____

_____

_____

_____

_____

_____

_____

_____

_____

_____

_____

_____

_____

_____

_____

_____

PRACTICE ESSAY EVALUATION FORM: STUDENT

Lesson Two

Evaluate your essay using the following criteria as a guide; a scoring section follows this chart.

Level 6	Level 5	Level 4	Level 3	Level 2	Level 1
Insightful - Outstanding	Effective - Solid	Competent - Adequate	Inadequate - Limited	Seriously flawed	Deficient
Convincing development of a position on the issue	Proficient, coherent development of a position on the issue	Workmanlike development of a position on the issue	Sketchy development of a position on the issue	Limited development of a position on the issue	Lack of a position on the issue
Selection of relevant examples and evidence to support writer's position	Selection of basically relevant evidence to support writer's position	Selection of reasonably appropriate evidence to support writer's position	Selection of weak or inappropriate evidence to support writer's position	Selection of weak or inappropriate evidence to support writer's position	Absence of evidence to support a point of view
Smooth, well-orchestrated progression from idea to idea	Relatively well-ordered progression from idea to idea	Acceptable progression from idea to idea	Erratic progression from idea to idea	Tendency toward incoherence	Absence of focus and organization
Use of varied sentence types and appropriate vocabulary	Reasonably varied sentence structure and reasonable vocabulary	Somewhat varied sentence structure and somewhat varied vocabulary	Somewhat limited vocabulary and inadequately varied sentence structure	Highly limited vocabulary and numerous problems with sentence structure	Rudimentary vocabulary and severe problems with sentence structure
Freedom from most technical flaws (grammar, usage, diction)	Relative freedom from technical flaws	Some flaws in mechanics, usage, and grammar	Multiple flaws in mechanics, usage, and grammar	Errors in mechanics, usage, and grammar serious enough to interfere with the reader's comprehension	Extensive flaws in mechanics, usage, and grammar severe enough to block the reader's comprehension

(Barron's 301, Kaplan 21, Official 105)

Level 6: demonstrates a clear command of writing and thinking skills despite the occasional, infrequent minor error.

Level 5: exhibits a generally dependable command of writing and thinking skills despite some mistakes.

Level 4: exhibits a generally adequate command of writing and thinking skills although the skills are typically   inconsistent in quality.

Level 3: exhibits an insufficient command of writing and thinking skills although the skills show some signs of   developing proficiency.

Level 2: exhibits a quite flawed command of writing and thinking skills.

Level 1: exhibits an acutely flawed command of writing and thinking skills.

Student's self-score of essay (between 1 and 6) _____

Read the following essay and then determine the score you would give it based on the scoring criteria and word count. Notice that the student worked through an outline, gave an introduction and a conclusion, but used too much time on these elements and could not actually write the body of the essay in the allotted time and assignment length. **Sample Student Essay**

Respond to the following statement:

Justice is an illusion in the minds of people who refuse reality.

<u>Assignment</u>: Consider the statement above. Decide on a position that represents your beliefs and write a persuasive essay explaining your position. You may use examples from history, literature, popular culture, current events, or personal experience to support your position.

Divine Justice in *The Brothers Karamazov*

Introduction: In *The Brothers Karamazov*, Dostoevsky outlines two attitudes toward divine justice and demonstrates that divine justice is mercifully inescapable. Ivan Fyodorovich, coming from a place of anger and confusion, despises the idea that the supreme God has the final say (judgement) in humanity's affairs and will eventually act in a way that makes amends for humanity's ills. Father Zossima accepts divine justice as freezing and is relieved that judgement of his fellow man is not left to him. In his youth, Father Zossima witnesses his friend Mikhail undergo the gracious and life-changing power of divine justice. Later in the novel, Dmitri Fyodorovich becomes the key example of God's working a man's circumstances for good comes.

I. Ivan- ("Rebellion") rebels against the idea of divine justice because he thinks it fundamentally cruel and sadistic for God to allow a child's tears to go unredeemed. Cannot accept a good God who allows a wicked world to hurt "innocent" children. Divine justice = unfair.

-experiences divine justice through guilt over his inadvertent murder of his father. This makes Ivan be genuine instead of hide behind philosophy and intellectual arguments—he loses the "one up" he had over God.

II. Zossima- ("From the Life..." and "Talks and Homilies") grateful for divine justice. Thinks it's fair and righteous; man's justice is unrighteous because all men are guilty "for all and before all," so they can't judge accurately. Divine justice = merciful and right.
-experienced it with Afansy and the duel. Walked Mikhail through it.

III. Mikhail- ("From the Life...") experienced it: though he wasn't judged by man for his crime, God knew his deed and didn't let his heart forget the crime. God's justice finally allowed his heart to be free from pent up self-loathing, guilt, and hypocrisy while saving his reputation and providing for his children (because no one believed he committed the crime). Divine justice = gracious.

IV. Mitya- experienced it: God spared him from endless baseness with a "blow of fate." Mitya would never have changed had he not been punished for his father's murder. He accepted the wrongful punishment because he had wanted to kill his father– shows that God's justice is concerned more with the heart than with physical actions. Since God sees the heart, man can't avoid his justice. Divine justice = inescapable and saving.

Conclusion: Through Ivan, Zossima, Mikhail, and Mitya, Dostoevsky masterfully explores numerous implications of God's ultimate control over man's decisions. The author sets up divine justice as merciful, though the mercy exhibits itself in ways that many would consider illogical or unwise for worldly success. He also demonstrates how unavoidable are God's purposes: the angry Ivan who threatens disbelief in God eventually experiences the trauma of God's justice in his life. In Zossima's, Mikhail's, and Mitya's lives, Dostoevsky follows this trauma with redemption. He does not, however, bring Ivan to a place of broken gratefulness to God; he merely sets up Ivan's experience of divine justice before closing his great novel. Perhaps Dostoevsky wanted readers to understand through Ivan that experiencing divine justice does not necessarily bring a man to repentance and redemption; a man can remain hardened or even can go insane after the experience.

_____

_____

_____

SAMPLE ESSAY EVALUATION FORM

Lesson Two

Evaluate the student's essay using the following criteria as a guide; a scoring section follows this chart.

Level 6	Level 5	Level 4	Level 3	Level 2	Level 1
Insightful - Outstanding	Effective - Solid	Competent - Adequate	Inadequate - Limited	Seriously flawed	Deficient
Convincing development of a position on the issue	Proficient, coherent development of a position on the issue	Workmanlike development of a position on the issue	Sketchy development of a position on the issue	Limited development of a position on the issue	Lack of a position on the issue
Selection of relevant examples and evidence to support writer's position	Selection of basically relevant evidence to support writer's position	Selection of reasonably appropriate evidence to support writer's position	Selection of weak or inappropriate evidence to support writer's position	Selection of weak or inappropriate evidence to support writer's position	Absence of evidence to support a point of view
Smooth, well-orchestrated progression from idea to idea	Relatively well-ordered progression from idea to idea	Acceptable progression from idea to idea	Erratic progression from idea to idea	Tendency toward incoherence	Absence of focus and organization
Use of varied sentence types and appropriate vocabulary	Reasonably varied sentence structure and reasonable vocabulary	Somewhat varied sentence structure and somewhat varied vocabulary	Somewhat limited vocabulary and inadequately varied sentence structure	Highly limited vocabulary and numerous problems with sentence structure	Rudimentary vocabulary and severe problems with sentence structure
Freedom from most technical flaws (grammar, usage, diction)	Relative freedom from technical flaws	Some flaws in mechanics, usage, and grammar	Multiple flaws in mechanics, usage, and grammar	Errors in mechanics, usage, and grammar serious enough to interfere with the reader's comprehension	Extensive flaws in mechanics, usage, and grammar severe enough to block the reader's comprehension

(Barron's 305, Kaplan 21, and Official 105)

Level 6: demonstrates a clear command of writing and thinking skills despite the occasional, infrequent minor error.

Level 5: exhibits a generally dependable command of writing and thinking skills despite some mistakes.

Level 4: exhibits a generally adequate command of writing and thinking skills although the skills are typically inconsistent in quality.

Level 3: exhibits an insufficient command of writing and thinking skills although the skills show some signs of developing proficiency.

Level 2: exhibits a quite flawed command of writing and thinking skills.

Level 1: exhibits an acutely flawed command of writing and thinking skills.

Student's score of sample essay (from 1 to 6) _____

[Based on the criteria, the assignment length, and the student's inability to complete the essay the score is 3].

LESSON THREE

DISCOVERING
AND
RECORDING
INFORMATION

A. Concepts

**Lesson Three
Overview**

1. Discovering and recording—notes and working bibliography

2. Limiting or broadening the topic

3. Designing the outline

4. Troubleshooting the outline

5. Considering a thesis

6. Coordinating outline, notes, and bibliography

B. Assignments

1. Collaborative learning interview: experienced researcher

2. Research language: *citation, plagiarism, summary, paraphrase, outline*

3. Research portfolio

4. Evaluations

5. SAT prep prompts: grammar, usage, diction—improving sentences; essay writing

6. Sample essay

CONCEPTS

DISCOVERING AND RECORDING INFORMATION

Documentation and Working Bibliography

You have visited and toured the library, met with the librarian, and become familiar with sources and resources in your library, including computer programs that will aid your search; you have determined the deadline for the project; you now know the general subject you will research, and you have a vague idea about a research thesis, enthymeme, or hypothesis; you know to research and write with your audience in mind—always. These decisions advance you toward the next step in your research strategy. This lesson leads you through recording research information, keeping up with where you got the information, and organizing the information into a system that will make the actual writing of your research a much easier process. Basically, you will learn note taking, precise source identification, outlining, and thesis revision.

Source

When you read information in a book, in a periodical (scholarly journal, magazine or newspaper), or on the Internet, or when you get information from the television, radio, or an interview, you are reading and hearing from a *source*. As soon as you read or hear the information, make a note of where you got the information; give necessary specifics so that anyone else can retrieve that information from that source. Record the information exactly as it appeared in the source (direct quotation), summarize the information, or give a paraphrase of the information so that you will know exactly what was said. Either way, the information must be accurate. It is not your information because you didn't think it or write it. Therefore, it belongs to someone else. Not to say who thought or spoke the information is the same as stealing that person's thoughts and words—taking them as your own—and that is called *plagiarism*. Plagiarism is a serious offense, is unethical, and is illegal. To plagiarize is to steal; schools, universities, and businesses take plagiarism so seriously that students and employees have been expelled, released, or penalized when plagiarism is discovered. For example, if you quote directly from David Dark's *The Gospel According to America*, you will quote the information exactly, including commas, capitalizations, and word by word rendition. Make a notation of where to find that quotation. After you've "taken down the note" from its source, you "give credit" to its author or speaker rather than claiming the information as your own. Any information that is not noted and is not general knowledge is considered yours in your research paper; make certain that it is.

Limiting or Broadening the Research Topic

As you continue searching computer databases, checking the table of contents and the indexes of books, looking thorough reference books, and scanning periodicals, you will begin to see patterns of information about your topic. You will see how some or all of the sources contain bits of information about particular aspects of your topic. These bits of information are what will serve as your research content. They are also what tell you whether or not you find enough or too much information on what you've chosen to research. If you aren't finding enough, you'll need to broaden your topic; if you are finding too much, you'll need to reduce or limit the scope of your research. For instance, researching "Guitars in North America" is too broad a topic. "The Vihuela Guitar of Spain" might be more appropriate. Likewise, researching "The Making of Martin Guitars in Nashville, TN" is probably too limited unless Nashville is the birthplace of Martin guitars. By this time you are limiting or broadening your topic based on available information.

Exploring a Thesis Statement

Searching, reading, and scanning in order to revise your research topic are also useful for exploring, refining, and declaring your thesis statement. For instance, if you propose to discover whether King Arthur was fact or fiction and you find absolutely no information about the possibility of his existence, you conclude that your research is incomplete, he is not an historical figure, or such a study has not been accomplished. Either you search deeper and perhaps more broadly or you abort this approach to the topic. If, indeed, there is no information about Arthur as an historical figure, you can then rearrange your thesis and write about Arthur as a fictional character. Your thesis has changed from: *Is King Arthur Fact or Fiction?* to *King Arthur is a Mythological Character.* Everything from that point on is from the perspective of King Arthur as a fictional character. You have refined your topic based on your exploration of information. Effective, full research is necessary when you draw these conclusions. Otherwise, you conclude in error, risk faulty research and a tarnished research reputation, and misinform your readers.

Designing a Preliminary Working Outline

While you are revising your thesis and searching for information, you are formulating notes that fit the point of your study. Keeping these notes in an orderly fashion will greatly enhance the writing of your findings. One of the most beneficial tools for this process is the outline. It serves as your road map for the entire project and prevents you from making unnecessary detours. It lets you know when you have too much information about one leg of your journey and when you don't have enough for the others. It teaches you when to subdivide information, when to abandon portions of information, and when to consolidate pieces of information. Understand that the outline changes and grows with the research. Indeed, you will have *several* working outlines as you progress through the project. Your outline will help you see how your ideas are flowing from one to the other, when they don't, and when they need more attention. It will help you see the logic, or lack thereof, in your paper. It's a good idea to save all variations of the outline (i.e. outline 1, outline 2, outline 3) so that you can refer to them as your research takes different directions.

Consider the following sample outline and researched thesis:

Thesis: The historical Arthur influenced both English and Spanish Literature.

    I. Historical Arthur

   II. Arthur's influence in English Literature

  III. Arthur's influence in Spanish Literature

This very basic outline subdivides its thesis and gives the audience the necessary information to know what is coming. The thesis provides the *purpose* of the paper: to *explain* the influence that King Arthur had on two major branches of literature. It also identifies the probable *audience* for the writer's perspective: *academicians, people interested in English or Spanish literature, and people interested in King Arthur legends.* As you see, this paper can address several audiences but is not geared toward the audience who is interested in why the guitar has a round hole in it. To draw the conclusions that Arthur is historical and that he influenced both English and Spanish literature, the writer has had to do considerable research. After this much research, no doubt she has begun filling in the sub-topics of the outline. Consider the next stage of the outline:

Thesis: The historical King Arthur influenced both English and Spanish Literature.

I. Historical Arthur

    A. Williams' *Annals Cambriae*

    B. Bede's *Ecclesiastical History*

    C. Entwistle's *Arthurian Legend in the Literatures of the Spanish Peninsula*

II. Arthur's influence in English Literature

    A. Ideal of the gentleman

    B. Revenge, forgiveness, and the gentleman

    C. Medieval tradition

    D. King Arthur of England's Edmund Spenser

III. Arthur's influence in Spanish Literature

    A. Dramas of honor

    B. Spanish romances of chivalry

    C. Spanish Golden Age

    D. King Arthur of Spain's Pedro Calderón de la Barca

Outline Points

Notice that this outline has three major headings. Each major heading has more than one subheading.

If there had been only enough information to form one subheading, that information would have to be included within another heading or discarded. In other words, if there is not enough information to support the heading, then it must be discarded.

If this researcher could find no source (or only one minor and poorly defined source) on the historicity of Arthur, the claim of an "historical Arthur" would be bogus.

From the accompanying outline we can determine that the writer of this research project is going to give information from three sources to back up the claim of King Arthur's historicity.

The writer is also going to provide four examples of Arthur's influence on English literature (major heading II), citing specifics from a poet, and four examples of Arthur's influence on Spanish literature (major heading III), citing specifics from an author.

Note the balanced, parallel structure in the outline and the movement from one heading to the next. Parallel structure means that you use consistent phrases or clauses or words throughout each point of the outline—not a combination of them per heading. Carefully laying out the points in the outline will facilitate the writing of the paper. It will also aid the transitions from one major heading to the next.

This outline serves the writer well in knowing where she is going; it also tells the audience what to expect. It demonstrates that enough research has occurred to carry the research to completion. Even though the outline will continue to evolve, the basics are present. It informs the audience of the purpose and perspective of the paper and guides the writer's structure.

Troubleshooting
the Thesis
and the Working
Outline

Lesson
Three

61

The previous example comes to fruition because research revealed sufficient information to give credence to the writer's purpose and perspective. But what happens if research doesn't show enough evidence to support the writer's purpose and perspective? For instance, what if the writer could find no information that King Arthur actually existed (or so little that claiming he did exist would itself be fictional)? Or what if the writer can find Arthur's influence in English literature but not in Spanish literature? Is all the effort and research lost? Absolutely not! What is called for is simply a renewed purpose and perspective. For instance, a revised preliminary outline might look something like:

Thesis: The mythological Arthur influenced English literature.

I. Mythological Arthur

II. Arthur's influence in English Literature

Then, as research reveals more and more information, the growing outline might look something like:

Thesis: The mythological King Arthur influenced English literature.

I. Mythological Arthur

A. Williams' *Annals Cambriae*

B. Bede's *Ecclesiastical History*

C. Brengle's *Arthur: King of Britain*

D. *Six Ole English Chronicles*

II. Arthur's influence in English Literature

A. Ideal of the gentleman

B. Revenge, forgiveness, and the gentleman

C. Medieval tradition

D. Arthur in Spenser's *The Faerie Queene*

This outline confirms the research from a different perspective and with a different *purpose*—to *explain* that King Arthur was indeed a mythological character who influenced the literature of England through *The Faerie Queene* by Edmund Spenser. Most likely the audience will be the same as that for the previous outline. Whether or not Arthur influenced any other literature would be beyond the scope of this research thesis.

Taking Notes: Coordinating Working Outline and Working Bibliography

A significant question at this stage of research centers on how to coordinate all the information that is being gathered. One traditional way of keeping up with information is to take notes on 4x6 inch cards. There are several good computer programs that can aid note taking also. However, for our learning purposes, we will use the more traditional method in order to understand the basics of coordinating research techniques. The 4x6 card will contain a notation that you hope to use in your project. The notation can either be a direct

Sample Note Card (4x6 inch size)

Written on this 4x6 card will be a summary of information from pages 85-87 of the book *Annals Cambriae*, written by Williams. If the information were a direct quotation, instead of a summary or paraphrase, it would contain quotation marks around the information so that later, after I've taken many other notes, I will remember that this one is a direct quotation. Note the **I. A.** in the upper right-hand corner. That code tells me that this note coordinates with point **A** under **Major Heading I** in my outline (see the outline below). If I drop my note cards and they get disordered, I will have a system for organizing them again. I continue with this process of note identification throughout my entire research project. Taking only one note on each card keeps the information clearly related to its topic and prevents my losing notes that are mixed in with other information.

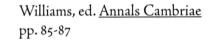

Williams, ed. <u>Annals Cambriae</u>   I. A.
pp. 85-87

quotation, a summary, or a paraphrase of the information you want to include. However, in the end, all notes that you take may not be appropriate to your project. Regardless of which kind of note you are taking, it is imperative that you write enough information about the source of every note so that you will be able to find the source and the information again. Additionally, coordinating each note card with its matching heading or sub-heading in the outline adds an element of organization. Study the sample note card on page 62 and the corresponding outline to understand the art and science of coordination.

Thesis: The historical King Arthur influenced both English and Spanish Literature.

Sample Outline

    I. Historical Arthur

        A. Williams' *Annals Cambriae*

        B. Bede's *Ecclesiastical History*

        C. Entwistle's *Arthurian Legend in the Literatures of the Spanish Peninsula*

    II. Arthur's influence in English Literature

        A. Ideal of the gentleman

        B. Revenge, forgiveness, and the gentleman

        C. Medieval tradition

        D. Arthur of England's Spenser

    III. Arthur's influence in Spanish Literature

        A. Dramas of honor

        B. Spanish romances of chivalry

        C. Spanish Golden Age

        D. Arthur of Spain's Calderón

    Now that you have coordinated this note with your outline, one more step remains—coordinating with a bibliography card. To differentiate note cards from bibliography cards, switch to 3x5 inch cards. Use a separate card for each book, periodical, interview, etc. that you use in your project. Put the cards in proper bibliographical form now, and you will save yourself much time and effort later. Proper bibliographical form is determined by which style manual you use. As stated before, if you are researching in the humanities field (language and literature), you will use the MLA Style Manual. If you are researching in the social sciences field (psychology, education), you will use the APA Style Manual. If you are researching in the field of religion, you will use the Turabian (or Chicago Manual of Style). Of course, your school, educator, or business may choose which style is preferred, and you will follow that dictate. For our learning purposes, the references and bibliographical entries in this book will adhere to the MLA Style Manual.

Sample Bibliography Card (3x5 inch size)

Since this card is bibliographical, it will not have notes on it. This card represents the place where you will find the information that is quoted, summarized, or paraphrased on its coordinating 4x6 note card. Both the note card and the bibliography card pertain to **Major Heading I Sub-Heading A**. Note that this particular source is an edited book that does not have a specific author.

Therefore, a typical bibliography card will look like the following one.

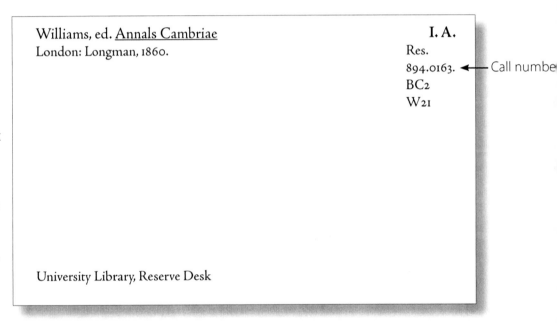

Williams, ed. <u>Annals Cambriae</u>
London: Longman, 1860.

I. A.
Res.
894.0163. ← Call number
BC2
W21

University Library, Reserve Desk

You now have a note card and a bibliography card that coordinate with your working outline. As your outline changes, make every effort to change the Heading and Subheading number and letter in the upper right-hand corner to make the cards match the outline. Doing so will keep your organization intact. This step is very helpful to the coherence of your project. By the time you have completed the research, you will have many note cards—perhaps as many as 75-100, depending on the length of the assignment—and you will have at least 8-10 bibliography cards, again depending on the length of the assignment. Remember that you have seen only one sample note card illustrated in this section. You will have several note cards that are identified for each Major Heading and Subheading. As your notes accumulate, merely add 1, 2, 3, etc. to each card. (For example: **II.C.** 4 indicates that this card is for Major Heading II, Subheading C and is the **4**th note for that section). You will want to balance, as much as possible, the number of notes you take for each heading and subheading so as not to have too many for one and not enough for another while making certain that you are adequately covering the information. Also, if you use one source in several headings, merely change the corner key on the note card to match the outline number and letter (e.g. a source might be used with I. A., II. C., and III. B.).

DISCOVERING
AND
RECORDING
INFORMATION

**Discover and
Record Information**

ASSIGNMENTS   1. Discover and record information

A. Read all the information in this lesson.

B. Continue library and Internet searches; you will be reading, scanning, and evaluating lots of information to decide what you will include in your research project.

C. Design your preliminary outline as you scan, read, and evaluate sources.

D. Take notes (4x6 inch cards) and begin coordinating them with the working outline.

E. Continue building the bibliography on 3x5 inch cards, being careful to follow the format in a well-recognized style manual (see Appendix H for a brief list of manuals).

F. Continue developing a thesis statement.

**Collaborative
Learning
Interview**

2. Collaborative learning interview with an experienced researcher. Enter into a collaborative learning experience by arranging for an interview with an experienced researcher (a teacher, pastor, college or graduate student, etc); plan questions for the interview; take notes during the interview; organize the notes. The purpose of this interview is to hear the research experiences of someone else. Ask about that person's experience with organizing research—what worked best and why for the particular type of research.

Step A: Call or personally arrange for a 30-45 minute meeting with the researcher. Courteously state your reasons for requesting the interview: you are researching a project and are interested in the person's perspective on organizing research.

Step B: Plan what you need to know, especially how organization helps with writing.

Step C: Write your questions, leaving enough space after each question to take notes on what the researcher tells you. Be respectful, sensitive, and courteous. You are taking valuable time which is being graciously granted to you.

Step D: Organize your interview notes; if they are helpful to your research, use them, but don't limit yourself if the interview results are not helpful.

3. Research language: Define the following terms using the information in this lesson, in the Appendix, and in a dictionary if necessary: *citation, plagiarism, summary, paraphrase, outline.* Add these terms, labeled and dated, to the Research Language section of your Research Portfolio.

Research Language

4. Research portfolio: Continue organizing your three-ringed binder with its 5 major divisions—Interviews, Research Language, Evaluations, Essays, and Research Project (See Appendix G).

Research Portfolio

5. Evaluations: Through evaluation you identify what you already know, what you don't know at all, and what you need to learn. Making these distinctions is part of the metacognitive knowledge dimension—higher-level thinking. Realizing what you don't know is one of the prerequisites for learning.

Evaluations

A. Both you and your teacher should independently complete a *Research Evaluation Form* and an *Essay Evaluation Form*; yours is located at the end of this lesson.

B. Compare the forms to gain perspective about your experience with this part of the research learning process and with the writing process.

C. Insert the forms into the Evaluations Section of your Research Portfolio.

RESEARCH EVALUATION FORM: STUDENT

Lesson Three

Student _____

Date _____

Evaluator _____

Concepts: discovering and recording information

	Possible Points	*Earned Points*
Concept readings completed	(20 points)	_____
Research portfolio organized and labeled	(5 points)	_____
Library and computer research continuing	(5 points)	_____
Note cards begun (student has at least 20)	(25 points)	_____
Bibliography cards begun (student has at least 5)	(25 points)	_____
Interview completed	(10 points)	_____
Student evaluation completed	(5 points)	_____
Teacher evaluation completed	(5 points)	_____

If you don't understand some of the concepts in this lesson, review them before you move to the next step.

Student's Self-Score for *Lesson Three* _____

6. SAT Preparation Prompts

The following SAT section will help prepare you for the Scholastic Aptitude Test, a standard college entrance exam. In 2005 the SAT was revised to include additional requirements in the English field. Completing these sections in each lesson will help prepare you for this test and will also enhance your thinking and writing skills. According to *The Official SAT Study Guide for the New SAT* (99), there are three types of multiple-choice questions: identifying sentence errors, improving sentences, and improving paragraphs. Forty-nine questions on grammar and usage test your ability to use language in a consistently clear manner and to improve writing by the use of revision and editing. The multiple-choice questions don't ask you to define or use grammatical terms and don't test spelling or capitalization. Punctuation helps you know the correct answer. Because of these additions to the SAT, this curriculum includes practice with identifying sentence errors and improving sentences.

Grammar, diction, and usage equals two-thirds of your writing score on the SAT. The essay portion equals the other one-third.

Some or all parts of the following sentences are underlined. The first answer choice, (A), simply repeats the underlined part of the sentence. The other four choices present four alternative ways to phrase the underlined part. Select the answer that produces the most effective sentence, one that is clear and exact, and blacken the appropriate space. In selecting your choice, be sure that it is standard written English and that it expresses the meaning of the original sentence.

SAT Format— Grammar, Diction, and Usage: Improving Sentences

1. After the deaths of his favorite wife in 1281 and his designated successor in 1285; Khubilai turned increasingly to food and drink.

(A) After the deaths of his favorite wife in 1281 and his designated successor in 1285; Khubilai

(B) After the deaths of his favorite wife in 1281 and his designated successor in 1285: Khubilai

(C) After the deaths of his favorite wife in 1281 and his designated successor in 1285. Khubilai

(D) After the deaths of his favorite wife and his designated successor in 1281 and 1285; Khubilai

(E) After the deaths of his favorite wife in 1281 and his designated successor in 1285, Khubilai

(A)   (B)   (C)   (D)   (E)

2. Edmund Spenser's *The Faerie Queene* brought a revival to England's declining <u>interest chivalric customs were reinstated and reached their height</u> with the crowning of Queen Elizabeth in 1558.

(A) <u>interest chivalric customs were reinstated and reached their height</u>

(B) interest in chivalric customs were reinstated and reached their height

(C) interest regardless of chivalric customs were reinstated and reached their height

(D) interest as chivalric customs were reinstated and reached their height

(E) interest chivalric customs, were reinstated and reached their height,

(A)   (B)   (C)   (D)   (E)

3. Chivalry developed in England and <u>Spain but for Spain it was not quite as casual a development.</u>

(A) <u>Spain but for Spain it was not quite as casual a development.</u>

(B) Spain for Spain it was not quite as casual a development.

(C) Spain but Spain did not have quite as casual a development.

(D) Spain, but for Spain it was not quite as casual a development.

(E) Spain; but Spain was not quite as casual a development.

(A)   (B)   (C)   (D)   (E)

4. <u>Emotional repression, self-severance, and restlessness, these three reactions</u> are consistently present in Dickens' descriptions.

(A) <u>Emotional repression, self-severance, and restlessness, these three reactions</u>

(B) Emotional repression, self-severance, and restlessness; these three reactions

(C) Emotional repression, self-severance, and restlessness. these three reactions

(D) Emotional repression, self-severance, and restlessness, these three reactions

(E) Emotional repression, self-severance, and restlessness: these three reactions

(A)   (B)   (C)   (D)   (E)

**SAT Essay
Writing**

7. SAT Essay Writing

The SAT "assesses your ability to develop and express ideas effectively; [it] evaluate[s] your ability to do the kind of writing required in college—writing that develops a point of view, presents ideas logically and clearly, and uses precise language . . . [the essay is] written in a limited time, which doesn't allow for many revisions, so it is considered and scored as a first draft" (Official 99).

Use this curriculum to prepare for the revised edition of the SAT, which includes writing and grammar elements in addition to three critical reading sections. Use the following pages dedicated to essay writing; they will help you organize and write your thoughts into essay format. Evaluation forms follow: one for you, and one for the sample SAT essay.

Successful writing includes:

1. A clearly expressed thesis statement

2. Well-developed ideas with relevant and accurate supporting information

3. Good organization

4. Appropriate, accurate, and varied vocabulary

5. Variety of sentence structure (syntax)

(Official 106)

The SAT allows you 46 lines on which to write between 300 and 400 words in a persuasive essay. It is important to write legibly because graders will spend approximately one to two minutes reading your essay. They will not spend time trying to decipher your handwriting. Use your two pages wisely, not writing in large letters or leaving extra wide margins. Your goal is to persuade your reader of your position.

**Planning Essay
Three**

Allot three to five minutes to think about and plan the essay—choosing between contrasting statements. Understand the statement and take a position.

Write about the following statement in two pages; you have *no more than twenty-five minutes.*

Respond to the statement:

Outlining helps organize thoughts.

Assignment: The statement above implies that planning and thinking before any mental activity promotes successful results. Write a persuasive essay supporting, disputing, or qualifying the statement. You may use examples from history, literature, popular culture, current events, or personal experience to support your position.

Initial thoughts about this statement:

_____

_____

Do I agree or disagree with this statement?

_____

_____

Reasons/support/evidence for my position (why I maintain this position):

I. Example from history, literature, popular culture, current events, or personal experience:

_____

_____

II. Example from history, literature, popular culture, current events, or personal experience:

_____

_____

III. Example from history, literature, popular culture, current events, or personal experience:

_____

_____

These thoughts become the outline for your essay. Do not take more than three to five minutes to organize these thoughts. These first *three to five minutes are crucial to the thinking skills* you will exhibit in the essay.

You will need the *next twenty minutes to persuade your audience* of your position on the issue, to support your position as you move from idea to idea, and to use appropriate vocabulary and varied sentence structure free from grammar, mechanics, and usage errors.

It is important not to change your position in the middle of the essay because you won't have time to rework the essay.

You are now ready to write the essay on two sheets of paper. Your goal is to write between 300 and 400 words on the issue.

It is very important to *time the writing*.

Outlining for Organization
Essay Three

Your Title:

_____

_____

_____

_____

_____

_____

_____

_____

_____

_____

_____

_____

_____

_____

_____

_____

_____

_____

_____

_____

_____

_____

_____

Evaluate your essay using the following criteria as a guide; a scoring section follows this chart.

Lesson Three

PRACTICE ESSAY
EVALUATION
FORM:
STUDENT

77

Lesson Three

Level 6	Level 5	Level 4	Level 3	Level 2	Level 1
Insightful - Outstanding	**Effective - Solid**	**Competent - Adequate**	**Inadequate - Limited**	**Seriously flawed**	**Deficient**
Convincing development of a position on the issue	Proficient, coherent development of a position on the issue	Workmanlike development of a position on the issue	Sketchy development of a position on the issue	Limited development of a position on the issue	Lack of a position on the issue
Selection of relevant examples and evidence to support writer's position	Selection of basically relevant evidence to support writer's position	Selection of reasonably appropriate evidence to support writer's position	Selection of weak or inappropriate evidence to support writer's position	Selection of weak or inappropriate evidence to support writer's position	Absence of evidence to support a point of view
Smooth, well-orchestrated progression from idea to idea	Relatively well-ordered progression from idea to idea	Acceptable progression from idea to idea	Erratic progression from idea to idea	Tendency toward incoherence	Absence of focus and organization
Use of varied sentence types and appropriate vocabulary	Reasonably varied sentence structure and reasonable vocabulary	Somewhat varied sentence structure and somewhat varied vocabulary	Somewhat limited vocabulary and inadequately varied sentence structure	Highly limited vocabulary and numerous problems with sentence structure	Rudimentary vocabulary and severe problems with sentence structure
Freedom from most technical flaws (grammar, usage, diction)	Relative freedom from technical flaws	Some flaws in mechanics, usage, and grammar	Multiple flaws in mechanics, usage, and grammar	Errors in mechanics, usage, and grammar serious enough to interfere with the reader's comprehension	Extensive flaws in mechanics, usage, and grammar severe enough to block the reader's comprehension

(Barron's 301, Kaplan 21, Official 105)

Level 6: demonstrates a clear command of writing and thinking skills despite the occasional, infrequent minor error.

Level 5: exhibits a generally dependable command of writing and thinking skills despite some mistakes.

Level 4: exhibits a generally adequate command of writing and thinking skills although the skills are typically inconsistent in quality.

Level 3: exhibits an insufficient command of writing and thinking skills although the skills show some signs of developing proficiency.

Level 2: exhibits a quite flawed command of writing and thinking skills.

Level 1: exhibits an acutely flawed command of writing and thinking skills.

Student's self-score of essay (between 1 and 6) _____

Sample Student Essay

Read the following essay and then determine the score you would give it based on the scoring criteria and word count. Pertinent criteria points that support the student's thesis are in bold-face type. This student responded (with a 500 word essay) to the following SAT Essay prompt by using a literary work that she had read and studied.

Respond to the following statement:

Suffering is a part of life.

<u>Assignment</u>: The statement above implies that an ordinary or normal part of life experience includes suffering. Do you agree or disagree? Write a persuasive essay supporting, disputing, or qualifying the statement. You may use examples from history, literature, popular culture, current events, or personal experience to support your position.

Suffering in *The Brothers Karamazov*

The abundant and seemingly futile suffering in the world deeply disturbs Dostoevsky. The author conveys and addresses his disturbance through his character Ivan Karamazov. To reconcile the notion of an all-powerful God with unjust suffering, Ivan concocts a scheme by which the universal church, led by the Grand Inquisitor, usurps control of mankind from God and then deceives mankind into ignorant happiness. **Dostoevsky uses his authorial skill to present Ivan's case as plausible and convincing.**

Dostoevsky relates his ideas about the Grand Inquisitor solely through Ivan's **narrative dialogue** with his brother Alyosha. Because of this approach, **persuasive diction** is a key element in establishing the credibility of the Grand Inquisitor. Dostoevsky has the Inquisitor **speak with scholarly words** that imply a **thorough knowledge of Biblical ideas.** Through his **own diction**, the Inquisitor comes across as **confident in his ideas** and **qualified for his position** to lead the church in its crusade against Jesus. The Inquisitor's **passionate speech** also adds **authenticity to his character**, making his plans seem workable. He **speaks eloquently with pitiful, emotional words.** He uses these pitiful words when **characterizing the masses** of suffering, ignorant people he seeks to save. Dostoevsky's diction goes hand in hand with his characterization of the Inquisitor, the masses, and Jesus. Curiously, Jesus is **never directly named.** Dostoevsky merely **describes the people's reaction** to Jesus's presence, making it obvious that the Inquisitor's prisoner is Christ reincarnate. Just as curious is Dostoevsky's **omission of** Satan's name. The Inquisitor reveals his clandestine cooperation with "the dread and intelligent spirit," who is obviously assumed to be Satan, Jesus's Arch-foe (p 251). In his clever exclusion of Jesus's and Satan's names, Dostoevsky **adds power and mystery** to the Grand Inquisitor's scheme.

Throughout the Inquisitor's tirade to Jesus, Dostoevsky **laces symbolism and figurative language** that support the Inquisitor's purposes. The Grand Inquisitor **repeatedly references** the symbolic bread that Jesus refused to offer mankind but that the church now embraces as a tool to woo the masses. Bread represents mankind's physical needs. Dostoevsky exposes an apparent weakness or fault in Jesus's ministry when he shows that Jesus refused to satisfy mankind's physical needs. Therefore, the Inquisitor's scheme seems to compassionately benefit the needy mankind. Dostoevsky's **figurative characterization** of mankind as dumb sheep also bolsters the Inquisitor's cause. Dumb sheep need a powerful, almost dictator-like authority to lead and protect them. The Grand Inquisitor wrecks the Biblical image of Jesus as the gentle Shepherd by showing how Jesus actually rejects his authority over people. For the Inquisitor, this rejection translates into Jesus's not truly caring for his people. The church then gladly usurps Jesus's staff and wields it to numb the masses from their suffering. Through these **intense symbols,** Dostoevsky's **seriousness toward his subject** is apparent. The author obviously wants his questions about God's omnipotence over man's suffering to be understood. He gives particular **attention to setting up the idea** of the Grand Inquisitor and then **skillfully constructs the Inquisitor's character** so that the importance of his concept will not be missed.

_____

_____

_____

_____

Evaluate the student's essay using the following criteria as a guide; a scoring section follows this chart.

Lesson Three

Level 6	Level 5	Level 4	Level 3	Level 2	Level 1
Insightful - Outstanding	**Effective - Solid**	**Competent - Adequate**	**Inadequate - Limited**	**Seriously flawed**	**Deficient**
Convincing development of a position on the issue	Proficient, coherent development of a position on the issue	Workmanlike development of a position on the issue	Sketchy development of a position on the issue	Limited development of a position on the issue	Lack of a position on the issue
Selection of relevant examples and evidence to support writer's position	Selection of basically relevant evidence to support writer's position	Selection of reasonably appropriate evidence to support writer's position	Selection of weak or inappropriate evidence to support writer's position	Selection of weak or inappropriate evidence to support writer's position	Absence of evidence to support a point of view
Smooth, well-orchestrated progression from idea to idea	Relatively well-ordered progression from idea to idea	Acceptable progression from idea to idea	Erratic progression from idea to idea	Tendency toward incoherence	Absence of focus and organization
Use of varied sentence types and appropriate vocabulary	Reasonably varied sentence structure and reasonable vocabulary	Somewhat varied sentence structure and somewhat varied vocabulary	Somewhat limited vocabulary and inadequately varied sentence structure	Highly limited vocabulary and numerous problems with sentence structure	Rudimentary vocabulary and severe problems with sentence structure
Freedom from most technical flaws (grammar, usage, diction)	Relative freedom from technical flaws	Some flaws in mechanics, usage, and grammar	Multiple flaws in mechanics, usage, and grammar	Errors in mechanics, usage, and grammar serious enough to interfere with the reader's comprehension	Extensive flaws in mechanics, usage, and grammar severe enough to block the reader's comprehension

(Barron's 301, Kaplan 21, Official 105)

Level 6: demonstrates a clear command of writing and thinking skills despite the occasional, infrequent minor error.
Level 5: exhibits a generally dependable command of writing and thinking skills despite some mistakes.
Level 4: exhibits a generally adequate command of writing and thinking skills although the skills are typically inconsistent in quality.
Level 3: exhibits an insufficient command of writing and thinking skills although the skills show some signs of developing proficiency.
Level 2: exhibits a quite flawed command of writing and thinking skills.
Level 1: exhibits an acutely flawed command of writing and thinking skills.

Student's score of sample essay (between 1 and 6) _____
[Based on criteria and assignment length, evaluator's score for this essay is 6].

LESSON
FOUR

DISCERNING
AND
REFLECTING

**Lesson Four
Overview**

A. Concepts

1. Discerning quality, integrity, and bias

2. Discerning relevance of passages

3. Reflecting

    a. Topic

    b. Thesis

    c. Outline

4. Placement of documentation

B. Assignments

1. Collaborative learning interview: professional researcher

2. Research language: *index, quality source, integrity, bias, relevance, reflection*

3. Research portfolio

4. Evaluations

5. SAT prep prompts: grammar, diction, and usage—improving sentences; essay writing

6. Sample essays

CONCEPTS

**DISCERNING
AND REFLECTING**

**Discern Quality,
Integrity, and Bias**

As you research, how will you know if a source has integrity? How will you know if the information is presented without bias? How will you know if the source is reliable? Beginning or relatively new researchers sometimes don't give enough thought to these kinds of questions because they assume that if information appears in written form in a book or magazine, it must be accurate. Unfortunately, that is not always true. However, information exists to help you answer the questions about reliability and integrity (and so do librarians). If you are unsure or unfamiliar about a publisher, consult *Literary Marketplace*. If you want to check on the reliability of a book, try *Book Review Digest*. Typically, scholarly journals, unlike popular magazines, undergo reviews by experts, who provide professional assessments, before information can be published in them. Understand that when you use scholarly journals published by particular organizations, they will likely be biased toward their organization. You can account for that in your evaluation of passages you plan to use.

Discerning the Integrity of a Source

observe the credentials of the author
observe the reputation of the author among other authorities
observe the date of the information—how current it is
observe the reputation of the publishing house
observe the documentation via notation and Works Cited pages
observe the indication that the author knows the subject
(Hodges 465)

If you are citing an Internet source, beware of sites that fail to acknowledge the author, to honor copyright laws, to update their contents often, or to offer links to other reputable sources and reliable documents (Hodges 467). Understand that Internet sites do not undergo the rigorous review processes by experts that scholarly journals do. Additionally, Internet sites can change so frequently that verification of sources is often impossible.

**Discern
Relevance**

You will not be able to read all the books, periodicals, and other sources of information that you find throughout the research period. Mastering the art of scanning huge volumes of text is an exceptionally valuable skill. With each source, quickly scan the table of contents and index to determine how much of the book's contents may be useful to you. When you identify passages that interest you and that seem relevant to your topic, slow the scanning process into critical reading. Then, you can discern if that passage fits other information you've been collecting. Critical reading allows you to read carefully and to compare this passage with information from other sources. You are now participating in discernment and evaluation of textual information. By checking contents and indexes, you are also locating other possible sources.

Reflection

By now you have scanned and read a great deal of information, and it is probably screaming inside your head. It's time to think, to reflect, to organize, and maybe time to stop searching for new information and to collate what you already have. If you have exhausted relevant and available sources, set the searching aside and allow yourself time to assimilate what you have learned.

Spend time rereading your notes, looking through your working bibliography, spot checking for irrelevant material that needs to be tossed, and letting the natural divisions in your information materialize. Sit back and think—simply reflect on what you are trying to accomplish. Remember your *topic*, focus on your *purpose*, and visualize your *audience*. Are you still relating to each of them, or have you gotten off track?

Topic

Now is also a good time to determine if you need to limit or expand the topic. Is everything flowing smoothly? Do you have enough information to support each major heading? Do you have too much information? Is all the information relevant to that particular heading? Can your notes provide appropriate support for every subheading? Do you have too much information for some subheadings and not enough for others? Answering these questions advises you about how much more time, if any, you need in the library.

Thesis

Next, allow yourself time to question your thesis. Does it reflect exactly what you want to do in the paper? Does it evidence your purpose? What *is* your purpose? Are you explaining, describing, arguing, or persuading? Does it clarify your perspective as the writer of this research? What *is* your perspective about this topic? If these elements are not clear in the thesis, now is an excellent time to revise and refine it. Clearly define your audience and purpose in the thesis.

Outline

Another element worthy of reflection is how your working outline is transforming into the final outline. Is it ready for this step? Does it coordinate with your thesis? When you make changes in the thesis, remember to adjust the outline. Is your outline synchronized with your note cards and working bibliography?

Verify Placement of Documentation

You have given yourself time to reflect on content. Now check for placement of documentation in every instance where you have quoted directly, summarized, or paraphrased information from a source. If you have done well with note cards, you have all the information you need to fill in any gaps that you spot. Lessons Five and Six will address the issue of style and form for documentation in notes and bibliographical entries.

This week of research preparation is crucial to the final product. So far, you have not actually written the paper. You have been preparing for the writing, much like a painter who carefully prepares the surface before he begins to paint. Preliminary preparation helps ensure a quality finish. If you have prepared well, your writing will go more smoothly.

DISCERNING AND REFLECTING

1. Continue research processes: discovering, recording, discerning, and reflecting on information

A. Read all the information in this lesson; scan previous lessons as a refresher.

B. Spend several hours discerning the quality and relevance of information you cite; scanning tables of contents and indexes to find additional information; reading and organizing, and most importantly, reflecting on the status of your paper and its audience and purpose.

C. Reflect on your topic.

D. Reflect on your thesis statement.

E. Reflect on your preliminary outline.

F. Coordinate outline, notes, and working bibliography.

G. Verify placement of notes.

2. Collaborative learning interview with a professional researcher. Enter into a collaborative learning experience by arranging for an interview with a professional researcher (an author, scientist, newspaper columnist, or business person, etc.); plan questions for the interview; take notes during the interview; organize the notes. The purpose of this interview is to hear the discernment experiences of a research professional.

Step A: Call or personally arrange for a 30-45 minute meeting with the professional. Courteously state your reasons for requesting the interview: you are researching a project and are interested in the professional's perspective on discerning quality and integrity in research.

Step B: Plan what you need to know, especially details about how to reflect and discern.

Step C: Write your questions, leaving enough space after each question to take notes on what the professional tells you. Be respectful, sensitive, and courteous. You are taking valuable time which is being graciously granted to you.

Step D: Organize your interview; if it is helpful for writing your first draft, use it, but don't limit yourself if the interview results are not helpful

Evaluations

3. Evaluations: Through evaluation you identify what you already know, what you don't know at all, and what you need to learn. Making these distinctions is part of the metacognitive knowledge dimension—higher-level thinking. Realizing what you don't know is one of the prerequisites for learning.

A. Both you and your teacher should independently complete a *Research Evaluation Form* and an *Essay Evaluation Form*; yours is located at the end of this lesson.

B. Compare the forms to gain perspective about your experience with this part of the research learning process and with the writing process.

C. Insert the forms into the Evaluations Section of your Research Portfolio.

Research Language

4. Research Language: Define the following terms using the information in this lesson, in the Appendix, and in a dictionary if necessary: *index, quality source, integrity, bias, relevance, reflection.* Add these terms, labeled and dated, to the Research Language section of your Research Portfolio.

Research Portfolio

5. Research Portfolio: Continue organizing and labeling your three-ringed binder with its 5 major divisions—Interviews, Research Language, Evaluations, Essays, and Research Project. (See Appendix G)

RESEARCH
EVALUATION
FORM:
STUDENT

Lesson Four

Student _____

Date _____

Evaluator _____

Concepts: discerning and reflecting

	Possible Points	Earned Points
Readings of concepts completed	(20 points)	_____
Research portfolio organized and labeled	(5 points)	_____
Notes cards accumulated (student has 80-100 notes)	(20 points)	_____
Working bibliography accumulated and checked for appropriate style and format (student has 10-14 bibliography cards)	(20 points)	_____
Evidence for reflection	(10 points)	_____
Thesis statement refined	(5 points)	_____
Interview completed	(10 points)	_____
Student evaluation completed	(5 points)	_____
Teacher evaluation completed	(5 points)	_____

If you don't fully understand the concepts in this lesson, please review them before you move to the next step.

Student's Self-Score for *Lesson Four* _____

**SAT
Preparation
Prompts**

6. SAT Preparation Prompts

The following SAT section will help prepare you for the Scholastic Aptitude Test, a standard college entrance exam. In 2005 the SAT was revised to include additional requirements in the English field. Completing these sections in each lesson will help prepare you for this test and will also enhance your thinking and writing skills. According to *The Official SAT Study Guide for the New SAT* (99), there are three types of multiple-choice questions: identifying sentence errors, improving sentences, and improving paragraphs. Forty-nine questions on grammar and usage test your ability to use language in a consistently clear manner and to improve writing by the use of revision and editing. The multiple-choice questions don't ask you to define or use grammatical terms and don't test spelling or capitalization. Punctuation helps you know the correct answer. Because of these additions to the SAT test, this curriculum includes practice with identifying sentence errors and improving sentences.

Grammar, diction, and usage equals two-thirds of your writing score on the SAT. The essay portion equals the other one-third.

**Grammar,
Diction, and
Usage: Improving
Sentences**

Some or all parts of the following sentence are underlined. The first answer choice, (A), simply repeats the underlined part of the sentence. The other four choices present four alternative ways to phrase the underlined part. Select the answer that produces the most effective sentence, one that is clear and exact, and blacken the appropriate space. In selecting your choice, be sure that it is standard written English, and that it expresses the meaning of the original sentence.

1. <u>England produced a national figure in Arthur though he may not have
been quite as magnificent a figure as the literary myths proclaim, he was
indeed an historical fact.</u>

(A) <u>England produced a national figure in Arthur though he may not have
been quite as magnificent a figure as the literary myths proclaim, he was
indeed an historical fact.</u>

(B) England produced a national figure in Arthur; Though he may not have
been quite as magnificent a figure as the literary myths proclaim, he was
indeed an historical fact.

(C) England produced a national figure in Arthur, though he may not have
been quite as magnificent a figure as the literary myths proclaim, he was
indeed an historical fact.

(D) England produced a national figure in Arthur and though he may not
have been quite as magnificent a figure as the literary myths proclaim, he was
indeed an historical fact.

(E) England produced a national figure in Arthur. Though he may not have
been quite as magnificent a figure as the literary myths proclaim, he was
indeed an historical fact.

(A)   (B)   (C)   (D)   (E)

2. Becoming a delegator-emperor was one of <u>Khubilai's wisest decisions: for he was free</u> to concentrate on domestic policy while Bayan commanded the army.

(A) <u>Khubilai's wisest decisions: for he was free</u>

(B) Khubilai's wisest decisions. for he was free

(C) Khubilai's wisest decisions, for he was free

(D) Khubilai's wisest decisions; For he was free

(E) Khubilai's wisest decisions, he was free

(A)   (B)   (C)   (D)   (E)

3. Like Charles Darnay, <u>Dickens stifles the frail remembrances of neglect and rejection, as a child,</u> he nurses intense resentment toward his parents for financial and emotional neglect.

(A) <u>Dickens stifles the frail remembrances of neglect and rejection, as a child,</u>

(B) Dickens stifles the frail remembrances of neglect and rejection. As a child,

(C) Dickens stifles the frail remembrances of neglect and rejection; As a child,

(D) Dickens stifles the frail remembrances of neglect and rejection as a child,

(E) Dickens stifles the frail remembrances of neglect and rejection. as a child,

(A)   (B)   (C)   (D)   (E)

4. The themes of <u>searching for something long lost, or something that might have been</u> show up in the author's works and personal life.

(A) <u>searching for something long lost, or something that might have been</u>

(B) searching for something long lost or something that might have been

(C) searching for something long lost; or something that might have been

(D) searching for something long lost. Or something that might have been

(E) searching for something long lost. Something that might have been

(A)   (B)   (C)   (D)   (E)

SAT Essay Writing

7. SAT Essay Writing

The SAT "assesses your ability to develop and express ideas effectively; [it] evaluate[s] your ability to do the kind of writing required in college—writing that develops a point of view, presents ideas logically and clearly, and uses precise language . . . [the essay is] written in a limited time, which doesn't allow for many revisions, so it is considered and scored as a first draft" (Official 99).

Use this curriculum to prepare for the revised edition of the SAT, which includes writing and grammar elements in addition to three critical reading sections. Use the following pages dedicated to essay writing; they will help you organize and write your thoughts into essay format. Evaluation forms follow: one for you, and one for the sample SAT essay.

Successful writing includes:

1. A clearly expressed thesis statement
2. Well-developed ideas with relevant and accurate supporting information
3. Good organization
4. Appropriate, accurate, and varied vocabulary
5. Variety of sentence structure (syntax)

   (Official 106)

The SAT allows you 46 lines on which to write between 300 and 400 words in a persuasive essay. It is important to write legibly because graders will spend approximately one to two minutes reading your essay. They will not spend time trying to decipher your handwriting. Use your two pages wisely, not writing in large letters or leaving extra wide margins. Your goal is to persuade your reader of your position.

Planning Essay Four

Allot three to five minutes to think about and plan the essay—choosing between two contrasting statements. Understand the statements and take a position.

In two pages write about your position on one of the following statements; you have *no more than twenty-five minutes*.

Choose between contrasting statements:

Writing as a creative expression allows the author total freedom of expression.

Writing as a careful discipline allows the author responsible freedom of expression.

<u>Assignment</u>: Consider the contrasting statements above. Choose the one that best represents your beliefs and write a persuasive essay explaining your choice. You may use examples from history, literature, popular culture, current events, or personal experience to support your position.

Initial thoughts about this statement:

_____

_____

Do I agree or disagree with this statement?

_____

_____

Reasons/support/evidence for my position (why I maintain this position):

I. Example from history, literature, popular culture, current events, or personal experience:

_____

_____

II. Example from history, literature, popular culture, current events, or personal experience:

_____

_____

III. Example from history, literature, popular culture, current events, or personal experience:

_____

_____

These thoughts become the outline for your essay. Do not take more than three to five min-utes to organize these thoughts. These first *three to five minutes are crucial to the thinking skills* you will exhibit in the essay.

You will need the *next twenty minutes to persuade your audience* of your position on the issue, to support your position as you move from idea to idea, and to use appropriate vocabulary and varied sentence structure free from grammar, mechanics, and usage errors.

It is important not to change your position in the middle of the essay because you won't have time to rework the essay.

You are now ready to write the essay on two sheets of paper. Your goal is to write between 300 and 400 words on the issue.

It is very important to *time the writing*.

Writing and Freedom of Expression
Essay Four

Your Title:

_____

_____

_____

_____

_____

_____

_____

_____

_____

_____

_____

_____

_____

_____

_____

_____

_____

_____

_____

_____

_____

Evaluate your essay using the following criteria as a guide; a scoring section follows this chart.

Lesson Four

Level 6	Level 5	Level 4	Level 3	Level 2	Level 1
Insightful - Outstanding	Effective - Solid	Competent - Adequate	Inadequate - Limited	Seriously flawed	Deficient
Convincing development of a position on the issue	Proficient, coherent development of a position on the issue	Workmanlike development of a position on the issue	Sketchy development of a position on the issue	Limited development of a position on the issue	Lack of a position on the issue
Selection of relevant examples and evidence to support writer's position	Selection of basically relevant evidence to support writer's position	Selection of reasonably appropriate evidence to support writer's position	Selection of weak or inappropriate evidence to support writer's position	Selection of weak or inappropriate evidence to support writer's position	Absence of evidence to support a point of view
Smooth, well-orchestrated progression from idea to idea	Relatively well-ordered progression from idea to idea	Acceptable progression from idea to idea	Erratic progression from idea to idea	Tendency toward incoherence	Absence of focus and organization
Use of varied sentence types and appropriate vocabulary	Reasonably varied sentence structure and reasonable vocabulary	Somewhat varied sentence structure and somewhat varied vocabulary	Somewhat limited vocabulary and inadequately varied sentence structure	Highly limited vocabulary and numerous problems with sentence structure	Rudimentary vocabulary and severe problems with sentence structure
Freedom from most technical flaws (grammar, usage, diction)	Relative freedom from technical flaws	Some flaws in mechanics, usage, and grammar	Multiple flaws in mechanics, usage, and grammar	Errors in mechanics, usage, and grammar serious enough to interfere with the reader's comprehension	Extensive flaws in mechanics, usage, and grammar severe enough to block the reader's comprehension

(Barron's 301, Kaplan 21, Official 105)

Level 6: demonstrates a clear command of writing and thinking skills despite the occasional, infrequent minor error.
Level 5: exhibits a generally dependable command of writing and thinking skills despite some mistakes.
Level 4: exhibits a generally adequate command of writing and thinking skills although the skills are typically inconsistent in quality.
Level 3: exhibits an insufficient command of writing and thinking skills although the skills show some signs of developing proficiency.
Level 2: exhibits a quite flawed command of writing and thinking skills.
Level 1: exhibits an acutely flawed command of writing and thinking skills.

Student's self-score of essay (between 1 and 6) _____

Sample Student Essay

Read the following essay and then determine the score you would give it based on the scoring criteria and word count. Using personal experience, this student responds (in slightly less than 500 words) to an SAT Essay prompt.

Respond to the following question:

What are the primary influences on your life?

Assignment: The question above implies that outside forces have the power to influence your life. Do you agree or disagree? Write a persuasive essay supporting, disputing, or qualifying the statement. You may use examples from history, literature, popular culture, current events, or personal experience to support your position.

Faith Building

In an application essay, I recently wrote that my faith is not separated from other aspects of my life in a way that keeps it from influencing those aspects; rather, it pervades all the aspects so that my journey of faith *is* my life. Behavior, schoolwork, struggles, and circumstances are merely the trimmings to the central theme of figuring out how to live, believe, and act in this world. Obviously, my parents have significantly influenced my spiritual growth. I learned a thwarted and coldly legalistic Christianity until I was about fourteen when my mom, my brother, and I began attending a grace-embracing church. My father's spiritual impact on me was harmful and negative for the most part; he did teach me the importance of intercessory prayer, though. My mother has modeled Biblical maternity all my life, and I have

only recently begun to understand her dedication, humility, and wisdom. When my brothers

and sisters still lived at home, their conversations and behavior effected in me a desire to pursue

God. My oldest sister often took time with me to talk through God-issues, and for awhile we

prayed together every week for our church. Ranking next for spiritual influences is probably my

youth leader. We have accumulated several days' worth of discussions centering around God,

faith, and the world. Even when I was bitterly antagonistic towards Christ, I enjoyed being

around my youth leader. He accepted my doubts and anger and gently supported me through

hating God.

Many spiritual life-changing times occurred because of my church youth leader. He

patiently talked me through rage until a breakthrough in my faith came. Conversations with

a girls' group leader have also had monumental impact on my belief. Like my youth leader,

she, too, accepted my doubts and did not ridicule me when my anger melted to weakness.

Conversations are the main events that have positively influenced my faith. Other standout

influential events are troubles within my family, my time away from my usual school, and the

death of a boy in my youth group.

Today, I am a Christian, standing for the most part in the orthodox, conservative camp

when it comes to doctrinal issues. I believe in God, I can pray often, and sometimes I can

hear God when we talk. I know I need God, though that need frustrates my frequent anger

and belligerence towards Him. I do not "witness" or share my beliefs verbally with very many

people. Often I read the Bible. The parts skipped over by children's Sunday school teachers

interest me most, though even the very familiar stories challenge my mind when I think seriously about them. I love the Bible and the truth-saturated teaching it offers. If music gives an

indication of my present faith, Vigilantes of Love, Chris Rice, and Switchfoot should sum it up.

Evaluate the student's essay using the following criteria as a guide; a scoring section follows this chart.

Lesson Four

Level 6	Level 5	Level 4	Level 3	Level 2	Level 1
Insightful – Outstanding	Effective – Solid	Competent – Adequate	Inadequate – Limited	Seriously flawed	Deficient
Convincing development of a position on the issue	Proficient, coherent development of a position on the issue	Workmanlike development of a position on the issue	Sketchy development of a position on the issue	Limited development of a position on the issue	Lack of a position on the issue
Selection of relevant examples and evidence to support writer's position	Selection of basically relevant evidence to support writer's position	Selection of reasonably appropriate evidence to support writer's position	Selection of weak or inappropriate evidence to support writer's position	Selection of weak or inappropriate evidence to support writer's position	Absence of evidence to support a point of view
Smooth, well-orchestrated progression from idea to idea	Relatively well-ordered progression from idea to idea	Acceptable progression from idea to idea	Erratic progression from idea to idea	Tendency toward incoherence	Absence of focus and organization
Use of varied sentence types and appropriate vocabulary	Reasonably varied sentence structure and reasonable vocabulary	Somewhat varied sentence structure and somewhat varied vocabulary	Somewhat limited vocabulary and inadequately varied sentence structure	Highly limited vocabulary and numerous problems with sentence structure	Rudimentary vocabulary and severe problems with sentence structure
Freedom from most technical flaws (grammar, usage, diction)	Relative freedom from technical flaws	Some flaws in mechanics, usage, and grammar	Multiple flaws in mechanics, usage, and grammar	Errors in mechanics, usage, and grammar serious enough to interfere with the reader's comprehension	Extensive flaws in mechanics, usage, and grammar severe enough to block the reader's comprehension

(Barron's 301, Kaplan 21, Official 105)

Level 6: demonstrates a clear command of writing and thinking skills despite the occasional, infrequent minor error.
Level 5: exhibits a generally dependable command of writing and thinking skills despite some mistakes.
Level 4: exhibits a generally adequate command of writing and thinking skills although the skills are typically inconsistent in quality.
Level 3: exhibits an insufficient command of writing and thinking skills although the skills show some signs of developing proficiency.
Level 2: exhibits a quite flawed command of writing and thinking skills.
Level 1: exhibits an acutely flawed command of writing and thinking skills.

Student's score of essay (between 1 and 6) _____
[Based on criteria and assignment length, evaluator's score for this essay is 6].

**Sample
Student
Essay**

Read the following essay and then determine the score you would give it based on the scoring criteria and word count. The student is able to write beyond the 300-400 word assignment length because she has recently studied literary themes and can transfer that knowledge and experience to the prompt. Notice that she would have to write with small legible letters and narrow margins in order to get her content on the hand-written two-page minimum.

Respond to the following statement:

Fairy tales and legends introduce children to make-believe worlds.

<u>Assignment</u>: The statement above implies that outside forces have the power to open up different worlds to children. Do you agree or disagree? Write a persuasive essay supporting, disputing, or qualifying the statement. You may use examples from history, literature, popular culture, current events, or personal experience to support your position.

Cinderella and Ellen Foster Themes

Many children remember one narrow aspect of the traditional Cinderella story: Cinderella married a handsome prince and lived happily ever after. Many Cinderella story themes are realistic enough to appear in the ultra-realistic novel *Ellen Foster*. Ellen and Cinderella share several surprisingly similar experiences—from living in a harsh family environment and bearing too much responsibility as a child to finally being rescued by an independent party.

After the death of Cinderella's father, the stepmother released all her cruelty upon

Cinderella. The orphan was helpless. Through a role reversal of Cinderella's situation, Ellen

Foster's mother had offered her daughter some protection from the brutality of Ellen's father,

but Ellen's mother died, leaving Ellen in a situation similar to Cinderella's. Both Ellen and

Cinderella were helpless in the face of their oppressors and had to wait for either, in Ellen's case,

the oppressor's death or, like Cinderella, a rescuer. After her father's death, Ellen lived with her

aunt, Nadine, and cousin, Dora. Nadine sickeningly pampered Dora and excluded Ellen from

any familial bond. Unlike Cinderella, Ellen finally took control of her situation and walked

away from the favoritism and exclusion.

Cinderella's stepmother also demeaned her by forcing her to work almost as a slave.

Adult responsibilities robbed both Cinderella and Ellen Foster of the typical childhood. At an

age even younger than Cinderella's, Ellen struggled to provide meals for herself. She learned

to budget money for her own needs, for household bills, and for savings before her father

squandered the rest of the money in his drinking binges. Her father's death did not alleviate

any of her responsibilities, though. While living with her virulent grandmother, Ellen was

forced to work alongside adult Negroes in cotton fields. Additionally, she came face to face with

death long before most children do through the deaths of her mother, father, and grandmother.

Ellen assumed guilt for her mother's death; she then tried to ease guilt's accusation by caring

for her cruel grandmother. Though Ellen's tasks outweighed those of Cinderella, overwhelming

obligations robbed both girls of their childhoods.

Cinderella and Ellen Foster would not have escaped from their oppressive childhoods

if it had not been for the intervention of a third party. Cinderella's savior was the fabled

handsome prince, and Ellen's was her foster mother, "new mama." Both girls had nothing tangible to offer their saviors. If the prince had forgotten his mesmerizing dance with her, Cinderella's chance for escaping her stepmother would have been nonexistent. Ellen's offering of money for room, board, and some attention was piteously naive to her new foster mother. If her new mama had slammed the door in her face, Ellen would have had no safe place to stay. Like Cinderella, her chance for escaping oppression would have been crushed if her savior had failed her. Though they were rescued, Cinderella and Ellen both deceived themselves about what life away from their oppressors would be like.

Many adults never realize that their quaintly remembered bedtime stories and fairytales actually portrayed such themes as an abusive family environment, a child's helplessness, and the need to be rescued. *Ellen Foster* provides a moving medium through which to explore the themes of the traditional Cinderella story. The novel could be considered a Cinderella story with a modern, realistic twist.

Evaluate the student's essay using the following criteria as a guide; a scoring section follows this chart.

Lesson Four

Level 6	Level 5	Level 4	Level 3	Level 2	Level 1
Insightful – Outstanding	**Effective – Solid**	**Competent – Adequate**	**Inadequate – Limited**	**Seriously flawed**	**Deficient**
Convincing development of a position on the issue	Proficient, coherent development of a position on the issue	Workmanlike development of a position on the issue	Sketchy development of a position on the issue	Limited development of a position on the issue	Lack of a position on the issue
Selection of relevant examples and evidence to support writer's position	Selection of basically relevant evidence to support writer's position	Selection of reasonably appropriate evidence to support writer's position	Selection of weak or inappropriate evidence to support writer's position	Selection of weak or inappropriate evidence to support writer's position	Absence of evidence to support a point of view
Smooth, well-orchestrated progression from idea to idea	Relatively well-ordered progression from idea to idea	Acceptable progression from idea to idea	Erratic progression from idea to idea	Tendency toward incoherence	Absence of focus and organization
Use of varied sentence types and appropriate vocabulary	Reasonably varied sentence structure and reasonable vocabulary	Somewhat varied sentence structure and somewhat varied vocabulary	Somewhat limited vocabulary and inadequately varied sentence structure	Highly limited vocabulary and numerous problems with sentence structure	Rudimentary vocabulary and severe problems with sentence structure
Freedom from most technical flaws (grammar, usage, diction)	Relative freedom from technical flaws	Some flaws in mechanics, usage, and grammar	Multiple flaws in mechanics, usage, and grammar	Errors in mechanics, usage, and grammar serious enough to interfere with the reader's comprehension	Extensive flaws in mechanics, usage, and grammar severe enough to block the reader's comprehension

(Barron's 301, Kaplan 21, Official 105)

Level 6: demonstrates a clear command of writing and thinking skills despite the occasional, infrequent minor error.
Level 5: exhibits a generally dependable command of writing and thinking skills despite some mistakes.
Level 4: exhibits a generally adequate command of writing and thinking skills although the skills are typically inconsistent in quality.
Level 3: exhibits an insufficient command of writing and thinking skills although the skills show some signs of developing proficiency.
Level 2: exhibits a quite flawed command of writing and thinking skills.
Level 1: exhibits an acutely flawed command of writing and thinking skills.

Student's score of essay (between 1 and 6) _____
[Based on criteria and assignment length, the SAT evaluator's score for this essay is 6].

LESSON FIVE

FINALIZING, TRANSITIONING, DRAFTING, AND DOCUMENTING

A. Concepts

**Lesson Five
Overview**

1. Declaring the thesis statement

2. Finalizing the outline

3. Transitioning and drafting

4. Preparing notes for manuscript

    a. Footnotes

    b. Endnotes

    c. Internal (parenthetical) notes

B. Assignments

1. Collaborative learning interview: experienced writer

2. Research language: *draft, transitions, manuscript, parenthetical note, footnote, endnote, free write*

3. Research portfolio

4. Evaluations

5. SAT prep prompts: grammar, diction, and usage—identifying sentence errors; essay writing

6. Sample essays

CONCEPTS

FINALIZING,
TRANSITIONING,
DRAFTING, AND
DOCUMENTING

**Detail and Finalize
the Outline**

During Lesson Four, you spent significant time bringing your library and Internet research to a close and reflecting on the information you had accumulated. When you discerned a need for change, you made adjustments. You altered or deleted anything that weakened your purpose or failed to address your audience. You meticulously analyzed your notes for content and then did the same for your working bibliography. You critiqued your thesis statement and measured it against your working outline, again making adjustments. You reflected on the whole project, looking for a balanced presentation of information among the headings.

**Sample Detailed
Outline (See
Sample Research
Paper #2 in
Appendix I)**

Outline

I. Description of Millay's sonnets

    A. Influences on her sonnet writing

        1. The Renaissance and Romantic periods

        2. Shakespeare

        3. Donne

    B. Topics addressed by her sonnets

        1. Politics

        2. Time

        3. Love

II. The role of gender in the traditional sonnet

    A. Male-dominance

    B. Female suppression

III. Millay's approach to the sonnet

    A. Reasons she wrote sonnets

    B. Ways she challenged the traditional sonnet's male-dominance

IV. Criticism of Millay's sonnets

    A. Negative

        1. Before her death

        2. After her death

    B. Positive

        1. Before her death

        2. After her death

This week, conclude all research. Find those last elusive references and take notes on them if they are relevant; fill in any gaps that you noticed last week. As you take the last notes, detail the outline and finalize the working bibliography. Coordinate all these pieces.

Transitions

The detailed outline lacks one major component at this point—*transitions.* When you move from one heading to the next, you need to transition. When you move from one subheading to the next, you need to transition. When you move from one thought to the next, you need to transition. A transition is a signal that one thing is concluding and another is coming—one is phasing out and another is approaching. Transitions serve to connect without abruptly ending one thing before beginning something new. Words, phrases, sentences, and sometimes whole paragraphs serve as connectors—as transitional bridges between bodies of information. Reread the first sentence of this lesson: *During Lesson Four, you spent significant time bringing your library and Internet research to a close and reflecting on the information you have accumulated.* This sentence is transitional—it provides a brief summary of what you accomplished in Lesson Four in order to prepare you for what is about to occur in Lesson Five. Another sentence, *This week, conclude all research: find those last elusive references and take notes on them if they are relevant; fill in any gaps you noticed last week,* introduces you to this week's emphasis while referring to last week's work. Notice one more example, found in the following section: *Now that the pieces are finalized and coordinated, confidently declare your thesis.* Again, the writer is transitioning the reader from what was to what will be.

Study the following rendition of transitional connectors:

Transitional Connectors

Alternative	or, nor, and, and then, moreover, besides, further, furthermore, and
Addition	likewise, also, too, again, in addition, even more important, next, first, second, third, in the first place, in the second place, finally, last
Comparison	similarly, likewise, in like manner
Contrast	but, yet, or, and yet, however, still, nevertheless, on the other hand, on the contrary, conversely even so, notwithstanding, in contrast, at the same time, although this may be true, otherwise, nonetheless
Place	here, beyond, nearby, opposite to, adjacent to, on the opposite side
Purpose	to this end, for this purpose, with this object
Result or Cause	so, for, therefore, accordingly
Summary	to sum up, in brief, on the whole, in sum, in short
Repetition	as I have said, in other words, that is, to be sure, as has been noted
Exemplification	for example, for instance, in any event
Intensification	in fact, indeed, to tell the truth
Time	meanwhile, at length, soon, after a few days, in the meantime, afterward, later, now, then, in the past, while

(Hodges 303).

Lesson
Five

**Declare
the Thesis
Statement**

113

Now that the pieces of research are finalized and coordinated, confidently declare your thesis. From this point on, your thesis will not change. You've worked diligently to hone your thesis, which functions as the guiding light for what you write. Before and after writing each heading and subheading, glance at your thesis to check your allegiance to it.

EXAMPLE: Consider the development of the following thesis.

<u>Thesis questioning</u> (1): Is there a way to connect my two major interests—English and Spanish literature?

<u>Thesis thinking</u> (2): Much of English literature has a code of chivalry. Spain's literature has a code of honor. Is there something that connects the chivalry and the honor in the literature of these two nations?

<u>Thesis thinking</u> (3): Time to interview and collaborate with teachers in the areas of interest. What could possibly connect the chivalry of England with the honor of Spain? Chivalry has links with King Arthur. Did King Arthur really exist or was he only a myth? Did he have anything to do with English literature besides the "fantasy" stories that have been handed down? Is there any connection between him and Spanish literature? Collaboration is a key element in coming to these conclusions. Only extensive research can answer the questions.

<u>Thesis thinking</u> (4): After much searching, researching, scanning and reading, it appears that Arthur, whether real or mythological, may have influenced both English and Spanish literature. Which literature? Specific examples?

<u>Thesis statement</u> (5): King Arthur influenced English literature through the works of Edmund Spencer; he also influenced Spanish literature through the works of Pedro Calderón de la Barca.

Drafting
the Research

Just as you developed a working bibliography, a working outline, and a thesis, all of which evolved throughout the research processes, so too will the actual writing of your research paper evolve. Writing the first copy is called writing the *first draft*, *first* because there will be several others, and *draft* because this writing is the preliminary form of the finished product. No one can research and write a *first* draft that is also the *final* draft.

You may want to delve into the writing of the first draft by creating the introduction. However, some writers wait until their creative energies are flowing before they tackle the introduction. Focused free writing can help get you in the frame of mind to write about your subject. Often, students think writing the introduction is one of the more difficult elements of researched writing—it's too hard to think of what to write. If that describes you, wait a while and develop the introduction later. Instead, begin drafting by writing your finalized thesis where the introductory paragraph will be. Keep it there in prime position as a memory stimulator.

Now, read major heading one (I. A. 1. a. b. 2. a. b. 3. a. b. c., etc.) of your detailed outline, which includes all the notes you've decided fit that heading. Celebration comes when you realize the value of this outline. Basically, it's now time to use all the writing skills you have previously learned. In each paragraph you know to use a topic sentence with supports (supports come from the notes keyed to the outline); you know to engage your audience as quickly as possible; to quote, summarize, or paraphrase accurately from your notes; and to provide notations for any information that comes from a source other than your head. However, it is important to include your own thinking in the writing. Otherwise, your research paper will be a report of facts rather than a carefully researched subject through which *you* draw deductions and conclusions. You also know that researched writing is formal in nature, meaning you will not use "I" or "you" or contractions in the paper unless the nature of the topic warrants it. Clarify any deviations from formality with your instructor. You know to be devoted to your purpose and to your audience.

For now, the main goal is to get words on paper—words that come from all the research you've done and from all the decisions and deductions you've made during the past four weeks. Don't be too concerned with grammar, diction, mechanics, or usage at this point—just get the content on paper. These other concerns will be dealt with later when you edit, revise, and proofread the multiple drafts.

After you have drafted major heading one, stop. You need to verify and properly format the citations of your sources before you continue writing your manuscript.

This lesson addresses the issue of style and form for documentation in notes. (Bibliographical entries were initially addressed in Lesson Two, and Lesson Six will deal further with how to cite sources internally.) Allow yourself time to verify style and format for bibliography and citations. Several examples of documentation and their coordinating Works Cited listing are included in this lesson. However, the style manual you have chosen for this research project is important for this exercise. You will arrange and compile Works Cited and notation entries according to the specific requirements of the MLA, APA, or Chicago manual, depending on the field in which you are researching. While these style manuals bear similarities, they vary significantly and must be adhered to precisely. Check your format for variations between books and periodicals with one author, two authors, many authors, or no authors—some have editors instead of authors. Check for placement of periods, commas, abbreviations, capitals, date of publication, place of publication, page numbers—in short check every single letter and number in every bibliographical entry, verifying accuracy. Be meticulous. Do the same for every notation for every source cited.

Preparing Documentation: Placement and Form of Citations

Traditionally, documentation of sources within a paper has entailed a complicated system of notations for references. Documentation appears either in the form of *internal notes (parenthetical notes), footnotes, endnotes,* or a combination of these methods. Especially in older documents, readers see superscripted numbers—small Arabic numerals raised half a space above the final word in a passage that is quoted, summarized, or paraphrased from a source—which refer them to notes at the bottom of the page, hence, footnotes. The superscripted numbers can also alert readers to look at the end of the chapter or paper for information about where to find the source, hence, endnotes. Internal notes may be present, but they do not have superscripted numbers. Instead, they depend on textual wording and parenthetical notation to alert and direct the reader to the source. With some style manuals, particularly APA and Turabian, or the Chicago manual, all three documentation procedures can function in any paper.

The MLA style, on the other hand, adopts a less invasive method of noting sources. In this instance, less invasive means less obtrusive to the reader—fewer interruptions: MLA almost exclusively uses *internal notes* that are keyed directly to the Works Cited page, eliminating the need for a separate section for footnotes at the bottom of the page or endnotes at the end of a chapter or the text. An exception allows endnotes for information that the writer thinks ought to be included as explanation but is not necessary to the text. The presence of footnotes has become rarer in some manuals because of the difficulty of placing them at the bottom of the text's pages. However, in some cases, professors and businesses will require footnotes, endnotes, and combinations, so be prepared to follow their precise requirements and instructions.

Since *Writing Research Papers with Confidence* is represented in the field of humanities, it incorporates the standard MLA style of documentation. With that said, what does MLA style of documentation actually look like in a research paper? Several examples are provided below, but know that there are many other instances that are not included here. These examples will also help you understand how to meld notation information into the text of your paper. See Lesson Six for more citation examples within the text.

**Internal
Documentation of
Sources**

Presentation of the following internal notes is arranged by:
Example of *internal note* from work with one author, two authors, etc.
Explanation of *internal note*
Example of coordinated Works Cited entry
Explanation of Works Cited entry

1. Example of *internal note* (*parenthetical note*) from work with *one* author:

According to Edward Maynadier in <u>The Arthur of the English Poets</u>, the historical source of Arthur is found in the English conquest of Briton since "with the arrival of the Anglo-Saxons in Briton, the days of the last Celtic independence were numbered" (6).

Explanation of *internal note*:

The author and the title of the reference are included within the text of the research paper; therefore, only the page of the source is needed in parentheses. Notice that the parentheses follow the quoted matter and the final punctuation concludes both the quotation and the reference.

Example of coordinated Works Cited entry:

Maynadier, Edward. <u>The Arthur of the English Poets</u>. Chicago:
      Houghton, 1935.

Explanation of Works Cited entry:

This book has one author whose name is given in the order of last name first, followed by a comma and then the first name followed by a period. The title comes next and is underlined and followed by a period. The place of publication is limited to what is written on the book's title page and is followed by a colon; the publishing house is limited to the first part of the company (Houghton of Houghton Mifflin) and is followed by a comma; the publication date is followed by a period. The entry is flush with the left margin.

2. Example of *internal note* from a book with *two authors*:

In Spain this Arthurian Cycle is represented not only by <u>Demanda del Santo Grial</u> (<u>Quest of the Holy Grail</u>) and <u>Baladro del sabio Merlin</u> (<u>Shout of the Wise Merlin</u>), but many others (Chandler and Schwartz 161).

Explanation of *internal note*:

Since there is no specific mention in the text of the authors, but the titles of the books are mentioned, the parenthetical notation contains the last names of the authors followed by the page number. There is no punctuation between the author's names or after the second author's name and the page number. Note the period *after* the closing of the parentheses but not before.

Example of coordinated Works Cited entry:

Chandler, Richard E. and Kessel Schwartz. <u>A New History of Spanish Literature</u>. Louisiana: State UP, 1961.

Explanation of Works Cited entry:

No commas are necessary when the source has only two authors. If more than two authors are given, punctuate as in words in a series. If more than three authors are given, you can supply all their last names as listed in your Works Cited, or you can follow the first author's last name by et al. (For instance: Moreno, Caldas, Fornsio, Smithoz, and Barca OR Moreno et al).

Also observe that one of these authors has an initial in his name and the other has a full name. The second name is not reversed. Note the punctuation. The publication place is followed by a colon, and the publishing house is abbreviated as U for University and P for Press. Note that the second line of the entry is indented five spaces.

3. Example of *internal note* **from a** *multivolume work with one author:*

W. F. Skene concludes that it was probably in 428 A.D., and not in 449 A.D., that the English made their first permanent settlement in Briton (*Celtic Scotland* I: 151).

Explanation of *internal note:*

The writer has provided the author, but not the title, within the text of the research paper; therefore, the title and the page number of the reference need to be included in parentheses. This reference is from a multivolume work, and the volume number should be included unless the list of Works Cited includes only one volume. Notice that a colon follows the volume number, the parentheses follow the noted matter, and the final punctuation concludes both the summary and the reference.

Example of coordinated Works Cited entry:

Skene, William F. Celtic Scotland: A History of Ancient Alban. 3 vols.
    Edinburgh: 1886.

Explanation of Works Cited entry:

This source has one author with name and initial; the complete work is in three volumes; the publishing house is omitted because the book was published before the 1900s.

4. Example of *internal note* from a *book with editor as author*:

In <u>El libro del Cauallero de Dios que avia por nombre Zifar</u> . . . (<u>The
Book of the Knight of God Whose Name Was Zifar</u> . . .) there is a hero
who was "ever close to God, and God to him . . ." and who was "perfect in
natural intelligence, in courage, in justice, in good counsel, and in good
will" (Wagner 9).

Explanation of *internal note*:

Until readers consult the list of Works Cited, it is difficult to know that
this reference is from a book that is edited rather than authored. The
parenthetical note treats this edited book in the same manner as an
authored one.

Example of coordinated Works Cited entry:

Wagner, Charles Philip, ed. <u>El libro del cuallero de Dios que avia por
    nombre Zifar</u>. Ann Arbor: U of Michigan P, 1929.

Explanation of Works Cited entry:

This entry differs from a one-author book in that it is an edited book.
Also, the editor's name is followed by a comma, followed by the
abbreviation ed. Publication place is followed by a colon and University
of Michigan Press is abbreviated to U of Michigan P, followed by a
comma and then the year of publication followed by a period.

If there were no editor and the book had no author, the Works Cited
entry would appear as

<u>libro del cauallero Zifar (El libro del cauallero de Dios)</u>. Ann Arbor:
    U of Michigan P, 1929.

5. Examples of *internal notes* **from a** *scholarly journal***:**

C. A. Jones presents a vivid discussion of honor and its relation to the
drama (199-210).

OR

In "Honor in Spanish Golden-Age Drama: Its Relation to Real Life
and to Moral," C. A. Jones presents a vivid discussion of honor and its
relation to the drama (199-210).

Explanation of *internal notes***:**

In the first example above, the author is given, and since there is no other
work by Jones in the Works Cited listing, only the page numbers are
needed in the parentheses. In the second example, both the author and
the title of the journal article are given, so only the page numbers are
needed in the parentheses. The Works Cited information will give the
rest of the necessary information—publication place, press, and date.

Example of coordinated Works Cited entry:

Jones, C. A. "Honor in Spanish Golden-Age Drama: Its Relation to Real
　　Life and to Morals." <u>Bulletin of Hispanic Studies</u>, 35 (1958),
　　199-210.

Explanation of Works Cited entry:

This entry comes from an article written by C. A. Jones in issue number
35 of a scholarly journal published in 1958. Place quotation marks around
the title of the journal article, and underline the title of the journal. Note
the period after the title of the journal article and the comma after the
title of the journal. To designate that this journal appears in issues rather
than volumes, use the same format you use with a journal of several
volumes but without the *vols.* designation. Note that the publication year
is in parentheses followed by a comma, followed by the page numbers of
the reference. Note the indention of the second line of the entry.

6. Example of *internal note* **accompanying a** *long quotation***:**

As a shelter for knighthood, Edmund Spenser's <u>Faerie Queene</u> perpetuated the love of chivalrous deeds. To Ludowick Brysskett, Spenser said

> I have already undertaken a work . . . which is in heroical verse under the title of a <u>Faery Queen</u>, to represent all the moral virtues, assigning to every virtue a knight to be the patron and defender of the same, in whose actions and feats of arms and chivalry the operations of that virtue, whereof he is the protector, are to be expressed, and the vices and unruly appetites that oppose themselves against the same are to be beaten down and overcome . . . . For that I conceived [this] should be most plausible and pleasing, being coloured with an historical fiction, I chose the history of King Arthur, as most fit for the excellency of his person, being made famous by many men's former works, and also farthest from the danger of envy and suspicion of present time. (Schofield 143)

Explanation of internal note following *a lengthy quotation***:**

This note gives the author of the original source of the information (Edmund Spenser) which is found in a book by an author named Schofield. Since the research writer does not mention Schofield in the text of the research paper, the author's name appears in the parenthetical note along with the page number from his book. Note that the period does *not* follow this parenthetical note but instead follows the lengthy quoted material. Since this direct quotation is over four lines in length, it is indented and blocked from the left margin. Note also that it contains ellipses (. . .) indicating that some information from Spenser's words is left out. Additionally, the quotation contains square brackets to indicate the writer's clarifying addition to the quoted matter.

Example of coordinated Works Cited entry:

Schofield, William Henry. <u>Chivalry in English Literature: Chaucer,
    Mallory, Spenser and Shakespeare.</u> Cambridge: Harvard, 1912.

Explanation of Works Cited entry:

This Works Cited entry offers no new information from that which has been given in examples 1-5. It merely demonstrates the internal documentation of a lengthy quotation.

ASSIGNMENTS

FINALIZING,
TRANSITIONING,
DRAFTING, AND
DOCUMENTING

**Finalize
the Outline,
Transition, and
Begin the First
Draft**

1. Finalize the outline, transition, and begin the first draft

A. **Read** all the information in this lesson.

B. **Spend several hours:** declare the thesis statement; finalize the detailed outline

C. **Draft** the first major point of the outline.

D. **Prepare notes** for inclusion in the body of the paper.

**Collaborative
Learning
Interview**

2. **Collaborative learning interview:** experienced writer. Enter into a collaborative learning experience by arranging for an interview with someone who does a lot of writing; plan questions for the interview; take notes during the interview; organize the notes. The purpose of this interview is to hear the writing experiences of a *writer*.

Step A: Call or personally arrange for a meeting with the writer. Courteously state your reasons for requesting the interview: you are reflecting on all the procedures involved in writing and are interested in the writer's perspectives.

Step B: Plan what you need to know, especially why precision makes a difference in the quality of the writing. Ask about the writer's experience with details and precision.

Step C: Write your questions, leaving enough space after each question to take notes on what the writer tells you. Be respectful, sensitive, and courteous. You are taking valuable time which is being graciously granted to you.

Step D: Organize your interview; if it is useful during the writing of your drafts, use it, but don't limit yourself if the interview results are not helpful.

3. Evaluations: Through evaluation you identify what you already know, what you don't know at all, and what you need to learn. Making these distinctions is part of the metacognitive knowledge dimension—higher-level thinking. Realizing what you don't know is one of the prerequisites for learning.

Evaluations

   A. Both you and your teacher should independently complete a *Research Evaluation Form* and an *Essay Evaluation Form;* yours is located at the end of this lesson.

   B. Compare the forms to gain perspective about your experience with this part of the research learning process and with the writing process.

   C. Insert the forms into the Evaluations Section of your Research Portfolio.

4. Research language: Define the following terms using the information in this lesson, in the Appendix, and in a dictionary if necessary: *draft, transitions, manuscript, parenthetical note, footnote, endnote, free write.* Add these terms, labeled and dated, to the Research Language section of your Research Portfolio.

**Research
Language**

5. Research Portfolio: Continue organizing and labeling your three-ringed binder with its 5 major divisions—Interviews, Research Language, Evaluations, Essays, and Research Project (See Appendix G).

**Research
Portfolio**

RESEARCH EVALUATION FORM: STUDENT

Lesson Five

Student _____

Date _____

Evaluator _____

Concepts: finalizing, transitioning, drafting, and documenting

	Possible Points	*Earned Points*
Concept readings completed	(20 points)	_____
Research portfolio organized and labeled	(5 points)	_____
Library and computer research accomplished (student has 80-100 notes)	(5 points)	_____
Bibliography completed (student has 8-15 bibliography cards as outlined in Lesson Two)	(10 points)	_____
Outline detailed and finalized	(20 points)	_____
Thesis statement declared	(5 points)	_____
First draft of heading one completed	(20 points)	_____
Interview completed	(5 points)	_____
Student evaluation completed	(5 points)	_____
Teacher evaluation completed	(5 points)	_____

If you don't fully understand the concepts in this lesson, please review them before you move to the next step.

Student's Self-Score for *Lesson Five* _____

6. SAT Preparation Prompts

SAT Preparation Prompts

The following SAT section will help prepare you for the Scholastic Aptitude Test, a standard college entrance exam. In 2005 the SAT was revised to include additional requirements in the English field. Completing these sections in each lesson will help prepare you for this test and will also enhance your thinking and writing skills. According to *The Official SAT Study Guide for the New SAT* (99), there are three types of multiple-choice questions: identifying sentence errors, improving sentences, and improving paragraphs. Forty-nine questions on grammar and usage test your ability to use language in a consistently clear manner and to improve writing by the use of revision and editing. The multiple-choice questions don't ask you to define or use grammatical terms and don't test spelling or capitalization. Punctuation helps you know the correct answer. Because of these additions to the SAT, this curriculum includes practice with identifying sentence errors and improving sentences.

Grammar, diction, and usage equals two-thirds of your writing score on the SAT. The essay portion equals the other one-third.

The sentences in this section may contain errors in grammar, usage, choice of words, or idiom. Either there is just one error in the sentence or the sentence is correct. Some words or phrases are underlined and lettered; everything else in the sentence is correct.

Grammar, Diction, and Usage: Identifying Sentence Errors

If an underlined word or phrase is incorrect, choose that letter; if the sentence is correct, select **No error**. Then blacken the appropriate space.

1. <u>These Arthurian legend</u> became <u>of popular importance</u> to the English poets of the twelfth
       A   B

<u>century due primarily</u> to the Norman Conquest, which placed woman <u>in the influential position</u>
      C   D

of literary critic. <u>No error.</u>
               E

                                  (A)   (B)   (C)   (D)   (E)

2. <u>Because of this addition</u> literature was forced <u>to follow</u> the interest of the age and
        A   B

<u>to incorporate</u> more tales of knighthood and chivalry, <u>direct descendants</u> of the Arthurian legends.
      C   D

<u>No error.</u>
  E

(A)   (B)   (C)   (D)   (E)

3. <u>Since both knights adhered to</u> the Code of Chivalry <u>that mandated honorable and courageous</u>
            A   B

<u>acts,</u> Arthur and him initiated the <u>Knights of the Round Table.</u> <u>No error.</u>
     C   D   E

(A)   (B)   (C)   (D)   (E)

4. Because he cannot always <u>except</u> his <u>young, fragile side,</u> Darnay eventually <u>seeks restoration</u>
                                A   B   C

<u>by returning</u> to his homeland. <u>No error.</u>
   D   E

(A)   (B)   (C)   (D)   (E)

7. SAT Essay Writing

The SAT "assesses your ability to develop and express ideas effectively; [it] evaluate[s] your ability to do the kind of writing required in college—writing that develops a point of view, presents ideas logically and clearly, and uses precise language . . . [the essay is] written in a limited time, which doesn't allow for many revisions, so it is considered and scored as a first draft" (Official 99).

Use this curriculum to prepare for the revised edition of the SAT, which includes writing and grammar elements in addition to three critical reading sections. Use the following pages dedicated to essay writing; they will help you organize and write your thoughts into essay format. Evaluation forms follow: one for you, and one for the sample SAT essay.

Successful writing includes:

1. A clearly expressed thesis statement

2. Well-developed ideas with relevant and accurate supporting information

3. Good organization

4. Appropriate, accurate, and varied vocabulary

5. Variety of sentence structure (syntax)

   (Official 106)

The SAT allows you 46 lines on which to write between 300 and 400 words in a persuasive essay. It is important to write legibly because graders will spend approximately one to two minutes reading your essay. They will not spend time trying to decipher your handwriting. Use your two pages wisely, not writing in large letters or leaving extra wide margins. Your goal is to persuade your reader of your position.

Allot three to five minutes to think about and plan the essay—choosing between two contrasting statements. Understand the statements and take a position.

Planning Essay Five

In two pages write about your position on one of the following statements; you have *no more than twenty-five minutes*.

Complete the statement:

A great piece of writing can bring discernment about what may be hidden in daily life.

An example of discernment hidden in daily life but brought to light through the media is _____.

Assignment: Complete the sentence above with a fictional work from literature, film, or television and write a persuasive essay demonstrating how that story taught an important truth.

Initial thoughts about this statement:

_____

_____

Do I agree or disagree with this statement?

_____

_____

Reasons/support/evidence for my position (why I maintain this position):

I. Example from history, literature, popular culture, current events, or personal experience:

_____

_____

II. Example from history, literature, popular culture, current events, or personal experience:

_____

_____

III. Example from history, literature, popular culture, current events, or personal experience:

_____

_____

These thoughts become the outline for your essay. Do not take more than three to five minutes to organize these thoughts. These first *three to five minutes are crucial to the thinking skills you will exhibit in the essay.*

You will need the *next twenty minutes to persuade your audience* of your position on the issue, to support your position as you move from idea to idea, and to use appropriate vocabulary and varied sentence structure free from grammar, mechanics, and usage errors.

It is important not to change your position in the middle of the essay because you won't have time to rework the essay.

You are now ready to write the essay on two sheets of paper. Your goal is to write between 300 and 400 words on the issue.

It is very important to *time the writing.*

Discernment in Writing
Essay Five

Your Title:

_____

_____

_____

_____

_____

_____

_____

_____

_____

_____

_____

_____

_____

_____

_____

_____

_____

_____

_____

_____

PRACTICE ESSAY EVALUATION FORM: STUDENT

Lesson Five

Evaluate your essay using the following criteria as a guide; a scoring section follows this chart.

Level 6	Level 5	Level 4	Level 3	Level 2	Level 1
Insightful - Outstanding	**Effective - Solid**	**Competent - Adequate**	**Inadequate - Limited**	**Seriously flawed**	**Deficient**
Convincing development of a position on the issue	Proficient, coherent development of a position on the issue	Workmanlike development of a position on the issue	Sketchy development of a position on the issue	Limited development of a position on the issue	Lack of a position on the issue
Selection of relevant examples and evidence to support writer's position	Selection of basically relevant evidence to support writer's position	Selection of reasonably appropriate evidence to support writer's position	Selection of weak or inappropriate evidence to support writer's position	Selection of weak or inappropriate evidence to support writer's position	Absence of evidence to support a point of view
Smooth, well-orchestrated progression from idea to idea	Relatively well-ordered progression from idea to idea	Acceptable progression from idea to idea	Erratic progression from idea to idea	Tendency toward incoherence	Absence of focus and organization
Use of varied sentence types and appropriate vocabulary	Reasonably varied sentence structure and reasonable vocabulary	Somewhat varied sentence structure and somewhat varied vocabulary	Somewhat limited vocabulary and inadequately varied sentence structure	Highly limited vocabulary and numerous problems with sentence structure	Rudimentary vocabulary and severe problems with sentence structure
Freedom from most technical flaws (grammar, usage, diction)	Relative freedom from technical flaws	Some flaws in mechanics, usage, and grammar	Multiple flaws in mechanics, usage, and grammar	Errors in mechanics, usage, and grammar serious enough to interfere with the reader's comprehension	Extensive flaws in mechanics, usage, and grammar severe enough to block the reader's comprehension

(Barron's 301, Kaplan 21, Official 105)

Level 6: demonstrates a clear command of writing and thinking skills despite the occasional, infrequent minor error.

Level 5: exhibits a generally dependable command of writing and thinking skills despite some mistakes.

Level 4: exhibits a generally adequate command of writing and thinking skills although the skills are typically inconsistent in quality.

Level 3: exhibits an insufficient command of writing and thinking skills although the skills show some signs of developing proficiency.

Level 2: exhibits a quite flawed command of writing and thinking skills.

Level 1: exhibits an acutely flawed command of writing and thinking skills.

Student's self-score of essay (between 1 and 6) _____

**Sample
Student
Essay**

Read the following essay and then determine the score you would give it based on the scoring criteria and word count. Using personal experience, this student responds (in 385 words) to the following SAT Essay prompt.

Respond to the following statement:

Emotions call forth actions.

__Assignment:__ The statement above implies that internal forces have the power to influence your actions. Do you agree or disagree? Write a persuasive essay supporting, disputing, or qualifying the statement. You may use examples from history, literature, popular culture, current events, or personal experience to support your position.

Hopelessness and Guilt

I swallowed my tongue and lowered my eyes on my first mission trip. Scared to be in Washington, D.C.'s subsidized housing, I stumbled awkwardly into day camps. Guilt smothered my voice as I ate lunch with the children: I enjoyed a square meal while they nibbled our group's peanut butter and jelly. I was powerless to keep order during craft time. How does a young, shy, white girl keep twenty-five hyperactive black children from painting each other? And how does that girl help the crying child who points to her splotched shirt while her little friend says, "The paint won't come off. Just show your mom and get the beating over with!"?

A year-and-a-half of subsequent experience has opened my mind to responses other than hopelessness and guilt. As I have spent time with a nursing home patient, my limitations have smacked me with reality. For the deaf and mostly unresponsive elderly woman, I can do nothing but wheel her around the nursing home lake and stroke her wiry hair. I cannot restore

her memory, re-spark her personality, or return her to the family missing its grandmother. Sim-

ply, I can love, but not fix, the aged woman.

Ironically, her unresponsiveness is my tutor. She wordlessly reveals my inability to solve

the world's problems. The heavy guilt I felt for not helping all the impoverished children in

D.C. was uselessly paralyzing; embarrassment over having all my needs met served no purpose

but to inactivate me. The true purpose of such guilt is to lead me to gratefulness for having

constant provision; only then can I use the provision to aid others. The awkwardness confus-

ing my approach to children completely different from me needs not incapacitate me. The more

hours I spend with people in situations unfamiliar to me, the less communication is hampered

by our dissimilarities. In those hours, the personalities behind the stereotypes jump out and

surprise me. Faces and stories supersede statistics which report poverty, illiteracy, and lack of

proper care—the people themselves are branded onto my heart, replacing the imprint of guilt

and hopelessness. Remembering these people, my aged friend and the D.C. children, focuses

my approach to community service: I cannot eliminate the world's sufferings; I can only live

gratefully and responsibly, loving and serving those with whom I cross paths. _____

_____

_____

_____

_____

Evaluate the student's essay using the following criteria as a guide; a scoring section follows this chart.

SAMPLE
ESSAY
EVALUATION
FORM

Lesson Five

Level 6	Level 5	Level 4	Level 3	Level 2	Level 1
Insightful - Outstanding	Effective - Solid	Competent - Adequate	Inadequate - Limited	Seriously flawed	Deficient
Convincing development of a position on the issue	Proficient, coherent development of a position on the issue	Workmanlike development of a position on the issue	Sketchy development of a position on the issue	Limited development of a position on the issue	Lack of a position on the issue
Selection of relevant examples and evidence to support writer's position	Selection of basically relevant evidence to support writer's position	Selection of reasonably appropriate evidence to support writer's position	Selection of weak or inappropriate evidence to support writer's position	Selection of weak or inappropriate evidence to support writer's position	Absence of evidence to support a point of view
Smooth, well-orchestrated progression from idea to idea	Relatively well-ordered progression from idea to idea	Acceptable progression from idea to idea	Erratic progression from idea to idea	Tendency toward incoherence	Absence of focus and organization
Use of varied sentence types and appropriate vocabulary	Reasonably varied sentence structure and reasonable vocabulary	Somewhat varied sentence structure and somewhat varied vocabulary	Somewhat limited vocabulary and inadequately varied sentence structure	Highly limited vocabulary and numerous problems with sentence structure	Rudimentary vocabulary and severe problems with sentence structure
Freedom from most technical flaws (grammar, usage, diction)	Relative freedom from technical flaws	Some flaws in mechanics, usage, and grammar	Multiple flaws in mechanics, usage, and grammar	Errors in mechanics, usage, and grammar serious enough to interfere with the reader's comprehension	Extensive flaws in mechanics, usage, and grammar severe enough to block the reader's comprehension

(Barron's 301, Kaplan 21, Official 105)

Level 6: demonstrates a clear command of writing and thinking skills despite the occasional, infrequent minor error.
Level 5: exhibits a generally dependable command of writing and thinking skills despite some mistakes.
Level 4: exhibits a generally adequate command of writing and thinking skills although the skills are typically inconsistent in quality.
Level 3: exhibits an insufficient command of writing and thinking skills although the skills show some signs of developing proficiency.
Level 2: exhibits a quite flawed command of writing and thinking skills.
Level 1: exhibits an acutely flawed command of writing and thinking skills.

Student's score of sample essay (between 1 and 6) _____
[Based on criteria and assignment length, the SAT evaluator's score for this essay is 6].

Sample Student Essay

Read the following essay and then determine the score you would give it based on the scoring criteria and word count. Using literary allusion applied fancifully to personal experience, this student responds (in 585 words) to the following SAT Essay prompt.

Respond to the following question:

If you could spend an evening with any person, living or dead, whom would you choose?

__Assignment__: The question above gives you opportunity to explore whom you would choose to experience for a specified amount of time. Whom will you choose? Why? Write a persuasive essay supporting, disputing, or qualifying the statement. You may use examples from history, literature, popular culture, current events, or personal experience to support your position.

An Evening with Proginoskes

For many children, imagination is a best friend. They can have tea parties with invisible playmates or decipher the song of a gurgling brook. As they grow older and acclimate to the "real world," though, many children value make-believe less and less. Some stop exercising imagination altogether when they reach adulthood. They miss out on the mysterious spontaneity of fantasy and lose the lessons learned from imagination. I want very much to maintain the ability to muse on fanciful matters. Therefore, I have not forgotten my childish habit of talking to trees. I have little difficulty accepting the phoenix's strange reincarnations, and I see no reason to doubt the existence of mermaids. Every time I open an antique armoire, my stomach tingles in anticipation of possibly glimpsing Narnia.

How I long for a visit from Proginoskes! He is the ball of wings, eyes, and fire who introduces himself as a cherub in Madeleine L'Engle's *A Wind in the Door*. He is witty and standoffishly lovable; what is more, he is real in the story. I do not want him to be real only in a paperback, though. I want him to materialize while I am walking with my dog one day. His appearance would dazzle me with wonder and hope. Blurting out endless questions and exclamations, I would jump up and down in excitement and relief: it is true, after all!

It is true that one can tesser, or wrinkle, time and space to travel cosmically. It is true that Aslan redeemed Narnia. Proginoskes would reveal that Bilbo Baggin's dragons and dwarves are not mere fables; the Tower of Geburah really does house the weapons of Gaal, and the Wise Woman's cloak actually wards off wolves. King Arthur will return because the Old Ones have succeeded, and animals truly can talk!

In conversing with the cherubim, I would describe how fantasy often sustains me while waiting in long lines at bureaucratic institutions or when plans are frustrated by the technicalities of red tape. On gross grey days, imagining what the trees are thinking makes the clouds seem less desolate. Proginoskes would hear why I love reading fantasy stories. They richly color life's monotonous routines and offer vivid insights into the "real world." I do not delegate imagination to child's play; nor do I consider the output of imagination strictly fictitious. I readily recognize the harm in deluding one's self or in living in a false conception of reality. The world, its people, and its events should not be ignored or considered nonexistent. However, being a "realist" does not preclude fantasy and imagination.

I half-believe in Camazotz, Narnia, the Middle Earth, and Anthropos. They are the worlds written about by Madeleine L'Engle, C. S. Lewis, J. R. R. Tolkein, and John White. I want to believe in L'Engle's concept of kything, George MacDonald's trick-playing fairies, and Susan Cooper's immortal characters, the Old Ones. If the cherubim Proginoskes visits me, I will ask him if all these things exist. Are there four- or five- dimensional beings whose normal actions would appear magical to me? If not, I will be a little sad. Only a little sad, though, because they still have value as didactic stories. Is it really alright to indulge the imagination while not denying or dreaming away the reality of our physical world? I want Prigonoskes's assurance that I need not hesitate to embrace imagination. The cherubim's visit would delight my fancy, satisfy some questions, and turn into an enchanting story for other fantasy aficionados.

Evaluate the student's essay using the following criteria as a guide; a scoring section follows this chart.

SAMPLE
ESSAY
EVALUATION
FORM

Lesson Five

Level 6	Level 5	Level 4	Level 3	Level 2	Level 1
Insightful - Outstanding	Effective - Solid	Competent - Adequate	Inadequate - Limited	Seriously flawed	Deficient
Convincing development of a position on the issue	Proficient, coherent development of a position on the issue	Workmanlike development of a position on the issue	Sketchy development of a position on the issue	Limited development of a position on the issue	Lack of a position on the issue
Selection of relevant examples and evidence to support writer's position	Selection of basically relevant evidence to support writer's position	Selection of reasonably appropriate evidence to support writer's position	Selection of weak or inappropriate evidence to support writer's position	Selection of weak or inappropriate evidence to support writer's position	Absence of evidence to support a point of view
Smooth, well-orchestrated progression from idea to idea	Relatively well-ordered progression from idea to idea	Acceptable progression from idea to idea	Erratic progression from idea to idea	Tendency toward incoherence	Absence of focus and organization
Use of varied sentence types and appropriate vocabulary	Reasonably varied sentence structure and reasonable vocabulary	Somewhat varied sentence structure and somewhat varied vocabulary	Somewhat limited vocabulary and inadequately varied sentence structure	Highly limited vocabulary and numerous problems with sentence structure	Rudimentary vocabulary and severe problems with sentence structure
Freedom from most technical flaws (grammar, usage, diction)	Relative freedom from technical flaws	Some flaws in mechanics, usage, and grammar	Multiple flaws in mechanics, usage, and grammar	Errors in mechanics, usage, and grammar serious enough to interfere with the reader's comprehension	Extensive flaws in mechanics, usage, and grammar severe enough to block the reader's comprehension

(Barron's 301, Kaplan 21, Official 105)

Level 6: demonstrates a clear command of writing and thinking skills despite the occasional, infrequent minor error.
Level 5: exhibits a generally dependable command of writing and thinking skills despite some mistakes.
Level 4: exhibits a generally adequate command of writing and thinking skills although the skills are typically inconsistent in quality.
Level 3: exhibits an insufficient command of writing and thinking skills although the skills show some signs of developing proficiency.
Level 2: exhibits a quite flawed command of writing and thinking skills.
Level 1: exhibits an acutely flawed command of writing and thinking skills.

Student's self-score of essay (between 1 and 6) _____
[Based on criteria and assignment length, the SAT evaluator's score for this essay is 6].

DRAFTING,
TRANSITIONING,
WORKS CITED,
AND READING
ALOUD

A. Concepts

Lesson Six
Overview

1. Drafting from the headings

2. Transitioning between headings

3. Drafting introduction

4. Drafting conclusion

5. Drafting Works Cited from working bibliography

6. Reading aloud

B. Assignments

1. No collaborative learning interview this week

2. Research language: *transition, draft, introduction, conclusion, Works Cited, voice*

3. Research portfolio

4. Evaluations

5. SAT prep prompts: grammar, diction, and usage—improving sentences; essay writing

6. Sample essay

CONCEPTS

DRAFTING,
TRANSITIONING,
WORKS CITED,
AND READING
ALOUD

**Drafting from
the Headings**

Lesson Five was a crucial step in your research process. You finalized and declared your thesis statement; you finalized your outline; you learned the significance of transitioning between headings and major thoughts; you learned the proper technique to cite information that is not general knowledge—parenthetical notation; and you began the drafting of your paper. You may have chosen to delay writing the introduction, but by now you have written the first draft of major heading one. You are ready to complete the first draft of the whole paper, including the introduction and the conclusion.

This week you have little new information to learn. This week is dedicated to writing. As with any writing, getting ideas onto paper follows thinking, planning, and outlining. For this first draft, write quickly, getting all the information onto the paper. For best results and the optimum use of writing time, allow yourself several concentrated hours, taking *short* breaks throughout. If you write sporadically—a few minutes today, a few minutes tomorrow, and a few minutes day after tomorrow—you will spend too much time completing the process and produce choppier work that needs more revision. Sporadic writing causes you to forget what you were thinking when you last put pen to paper (fingers to keys). You will spend time rereading what you've written rather than writing.

You have already done the preliminary work that makes concentrated writing much easier. You have brainstormed and planned, collected and collated information, organized topics and headings, deleted information that did not fit your thesis statement, and drafted and revised several outlines. Now you reap the benefits of all that diligent work.

Follow your outline and turn those phrases and ideas into sentences and paragraphs.

**Transitioning
between Headings
and Thoughts**

Lesson Five also contained a boxed exhibit of *transitional connectors*. Refer to those transitions and incorporate as many of them as you need to make your paper flow smoothly from one heading to the next—even from one paragraph to the next. Remember those dedicated parents, teachers, and tutors who helped develop your early writing skills as they taught you about topic sentences, supports for topic sentences, and how to combine them into effective paragraphs. If you learned well then, you are better prepared now for this more sophisticated form of writing. If not, drafting the paper will require more concentration and perhaps some review.

Voice

On some occasions it is necessary to alter the *voice* of a formal paper from third person (he, she, one) to first person (I, we) in order to meet the assignment. Talk with your instructor to be very clear about *voice*. In the following paragraphs the student is presenting information from personal observation about plans that he will initiate; therefore, he uses first person. Read the paragraphs to observe how the student makes excellent use of transitions throughout his personal observations. Transition words, phrases, and sentences are in bold for you to easily identify.

Example of Transitions and First Person Voice in a Student Paper

. . . **Although** enmeshed systems offer a lot of support, those involved usually become too dependent on the system and have trouble functioning independently. Every family has a structure, and it is important in structural family therapy that the therapist actually sees family members interact with each other. Only through viewing actual interactions can a therapist be able to intervene appropriately.

My first supervised intervention will be working with interaction. Fortunately, I have already begun the process of joining and accommodating, since the family knows me from a prior hospitalization experience. While they may not immediately reveal their deepest, darkest secrets, we do have a basic foundation on which to begin work. I will begin by gathering the family together and asking Mr. Macklin to discuss his discharge plan. **In other words,** if Mr. Macklin were in total control, what could happen in the future? I will then give his children a chance to repeat the scenario as if they were in charge. I believe that at some point, a statement made by Mr. Macklin or the children will stimulate the others, and a chance for enactment will result. Seeing the family interact will give me the opportunity to further examine the family structure as a whole. **In addition,** the interaction will give the family members a chance to directly talk about an issue that both sides have purposely avoided discussing. Interactions force family members to work things out with themselves. While the family may have expected me to do all the work, I will only facilitate the conversation and allow them to reveal themselves.

Another intervention will involve structural mapping. **As mentioned before,** families often come into therapy with preconceived notions about what the problems is and who is to blame. **In this case,** the majority of the family will be "blaming" Mr. Macklin for his stubbornness and unwillingness to consider a safer discharge plan. It would be easy to gang up on Mr. Macklin and accuse him of being selfish and cruel in not considering the wellbeing of others in his decision making. As a structural family therapist, allowing this ganging-up action would be irresponsible.

As the family continues to interact, I will structurally assess their functioning. **However,** it is important that a basic hypothesis be formed before the therapy begins to assure that I don't become inducted into the Macklin family culture. In the formation of my hypothesis, I must keep in mind issues of class and gender in the functioning of the Macklin family.

The Macklin family is a working class family that follows a traditional blue collar pattern in which the father is the head of the family, and his decisions are not questioned. **In addition,** while the children may blame their mother for "wishy-washiness" and not having the courage to stand up to her husband, they are not taking into account the oppression that many women face in marriages and families. . . .

Now go back and reread only the highlighted words and phrases to get a better view of what transitions do for the paper—how they tie the elements together by making references back and forth to coordinate segments of thought. Remember that though this paper is written in first person, research papers are usually written in third person.

Drafting the Introduction

The introduction is your opportunity to convince readers that reading your paper will be a valuable use of their time. Convince them that you have something worthwhile to say and that the paper is easy to follow because of your organization. Readers will learn from the introduction that you are going to try to persuade them, to argue a point, to describe something, or to explain something that is important to you. Your thesis tells them exactly what that *something* is. Many writers position the thesis as the last sentence of the introductory paragraph. They present a broad picture of their topic, offer a "hook" to draw in their readers, and then taper to the thesis in the last sentence. This method is similar to meeting someone for the first time, working through general introductions, and then getting to know each other through more specific conversation. This method resembles a funnel—broad to narrow.

However, some writers position their thesis sentence as the beginning of the introductory paragraph and lead their audience through a reverse perspective. They provide the thesis immediately and then back out of it with logic to explain how they derived it. This method resembles a pyramid by beginning narrow and specific and then broadening. Still others work the thesis into the middle of the introductory paragraph with explanations on both sides. You might think of this method as resembling an hour glass—broad to narrow to broad. Consider your writing style, your audience, your purpose, or your teacher instruction when you position your thesis.

If, as a writer, you choose to compose your introduction *after* you write the paper, now is the time to do so. Regardless of when you write the introduction, check yourself for effectiveness, clarity, and specificity. Think again about your purpose and your audience, referring to Lesson Two to refresh your memory.

Note how the student begins with a broad overview for readers in the first paragraph and then narrows to the specific point of the paper, the thesis, at the end of the paragraph. The second paragraph serves as an introduction to the characters in the study.

Working toward Discharge

Example One: Introductory Paragraph in Student Writing— First Person

The agency with which I work serves in a local community hospital. As a junior intern, I am currently providing supervised services in the rehabilitation unit of the hospital. The hospital's rehabilitation

**Example One:
Introductory
Paragraph
in Student
Writing—
First Person**

unit is classified as subacute/intensive, meaning that patients must be able to participate in three hours of therapy a day. Throughout their hospital stay (an average of one to three weeks), patients work with physical, occupational, recreational, and speech therapists. While some patients are recovering from knee and hip replacement surgeries, the majority are recent stroke victims. Social work duties on the rehabilitation unit include initial assessments, conferences with the families, and assistance in discharge planning. (Thesis)

I am currently working with the Macklin family. Tom Macklin, the patient, is eighty-four and has been married to his eighty-one-year-old wife Jan for over sixty years. They have four children: Karen, the oldest, is fifty-nine, married, and lives in Lansing; Bill is fifty-seven, unmarried, and lives in close proximity to the patient; Barb, fifty-three, is a truck driver and does not live in the area; Bev, fifty, is married and lives close to the patient. Mr. Macklin has been referred to the rehabilitation unit of our hospital after suffering a stroke. His past medical history includes a previous stroke suffered in 1998, as well as the amputation of his left hand after a grenade accident in World War II. During the patient's early stay in the hospital, my main family contact has been with the youngest daughter, Bev.

Use the student's examples of introduction and thesis and determine

1. purpose of the paper (what is the writer going to do—explain, describe, argue, or persuade?)

2. audience of the paper (for whom is the writer writing?)

3. occasion of the paper (why is the writer writing about this particular subject?)

**Twenty to Fourteen:
Khubilai Khan's Thirty-four Year Rule over China**

By 1294, the four Mongol empires encompassed virtually all of Asia. Descendants of the great warlord Genghis Khan ruled the separate kingdoms, the largest being Khubilai Khan's Yüan Dynasty in China. Khubilai lead his territory differently than the other, more traditional Mongolian Khans ruled, and the result was a unified, peaceful China. During the first part of his rule, Khubilai struck a prosperous balance between the practices of his Mongolian heritage and those of his conquered Chinese subjects (Rossabi 115). This delicate act grew unbalanced later when Khubilai reverted to the personal extravagance and brash expansionism characteristic of his Mongolian predecessors. Through Khubilai's integration of Mongolian expansion and Chinese domestic policy, the Yüan Dynasty flourished before its ultimate decline from overexpansion and the emperor's overindulgence. (Thesis)

**Example Two:
Introductory
Paragraph in
Student Writing—
Third Person**

Constantly ask yourself if you are addressing your particular audience and if you are *persuading, arguing, describing,* or *explaining.*

**Purpose and
Audience**

After you have drafted the introduction and all headings, you will draw conclusions or offer solutions in a paragraph dedicated to this task. For research to be authentic and purposeful it must truly relate to your audience. Your audience must really want to know what you present, and you must satisfy their curiosity or questions. Whereas the introduction told the audience what you intended to do (the purpose), the conclusion tells them what you have done (the why and the how). The conclusion provides the audience with solutions or new information and brings to closure the purpose of your research. If your purpose has been to persuade, you will briefly reiterate the reasons you've used to convince them. If your purpose has been to argue a point, you will briefly review the arguments and their reliability. If your

**Drafting the
Conclusion**

purpose has been to describe, you will briefly restate major descriptives. If your purpose has been to explain, you will briefly clarify the major points. Do not use the word *conclusion* in the concluding paragraph and do not use the same words that you used in the introduction. The introduction and the conclusion have different purposes. Make certain that you understand and then clarify their reasons for existing.

Note how this student draws readers back to the thesis presented in the introduction, draws conclusions without needless repetition, and provides readers with the results of the research.

**Example One:
Conclusion in
Student Writing—
First Person**

The resolution of the Macklin family's problem is currently unclear. While I am able to offer several supervised interventions varying in style and substance, I am unable to "change" this family. A frustrating truth in family therapy is that if a family does not want to change, it will not change. However, I observe that therapists have the exciting opportunity to use their skills in order to make change an exciting and possible option for previously unreachable families. Though success is not always guaranteed, the use of these different styles of family therapy offers clients several options to join in a positive intervention process.

Even without reading the body of this student's paper, you know what he is doing in the paper by reading the introduction with its thesis, the transitions, and the conclusion.

**Example Two:
Conclusion in
Student Writing—
Third Person**

For twenty years, Khubilai provided strong, competent leadership for the largest Asian empire in the thirteenth century. He prospered his country's trade markets and treated lower classes with a fairness and a respect uncustomary to Mongolian rule. Khubilai would have been wise to seek Chinese counsel after several of his trusted advisors died, for the financial assistance from non-Chinese ministers burdened and alienated his subjects. Had he not given in to gluttony and drunkenness, Khubilai could have maintained the favorable reputation he earned during his early rule. Several failed attempts at expansion precipitated the financial stress which worsened as Khubilai's habits demanded increasing luxury. The Khan's personal deterioration, worsening financial situation, and thwarted military campaigns ultimately undermined the stability he had established in China during the first twenty years of his reign. However, in spite of a tarnished reputation, the Mongol leader still earned an influential position in history. *LIFE* Magazine mentions his Yüan Dynasty in recounting the "100 most significant events shaping human civilization" in the last millennium. After praising Khubilai's dynasty, *LIFE* accurately observes that "the size of the empire was ultimately its undoing, and within a few decades it began to fragment." The Mongols fell into the same trap that destroyed the empires of Alexander the Great, Rome, and Napoleon: overexpansion and overindulgence. Had Khubilai Khan been content to govern Northern and Southern China as he had for twenty years, perhaps he would have delivered to his successors the strong and unified empire that the Yüan Dynasty once was.

From Working Bibliography to Works Cited

The paper is drafted! Congratulate yourself! Take a few moments to revel in what you've accomplished. Pat yourself (literally) on the back and accept all accolades for this much progress. Researching and writing is hard work, and you've done a tremendous amount of both. Appreciate your proficiency and thank the Lord for your ability to understand and to accomplish one of the most demanding forms of writing!

Throughout the project, you compiled a working bibliography, a listing of cards for every source used throughout the research. Many of those sources became obsolete as the project evolved and you realized they were not needed. All the sources that *were needed* and *were used* make up the Works Cited. In other words, if you have a parenthetical notation within the paper, you must include the source of that parenthetical note in the Works Cited listing. Conversely, if a source is listed in Works Cited, you must use it as a reference somewhere within the paper.

If you carefully compiled the working bibliography, most of the effort for the Works Cited is complete. All you need to do now is compare parenthetical notes within the paper with the working bibliography. Remove all the references from the working bibliography that are not actually used in the paper. Be alert for any parenthetical notes that do not have a corresponding bibliography card. If you find any of these, you will have to retrace your research steps and find the source for that information or rework the material and leave out that information. Under no circumstances should you have unidentified or undocumented information. The remaining references—works that you are actually citing in the paper—should be alphabetized and properly formatted in either MLA, APA, or Chicago Style (see Lesson Five). Examples of other Works Cited entries are listed below.

Samples of Variations for Works Cited Listings

Barnett, Elizabeth. <u>Collected Sonnets of Edna St. Vincent Millay (Revised and Expanded Edition)</u>. New York: Harper and Row, 1988.

Boscolo, L., G. Cecchin, L. Hoffman, and P. Penn. <u>Milan Systemic Family Therapy</u>. New York: Basic Books, 1987.

Burch, Francis F. "Millay's Not in a Silver Casket Cool with Pearls." <u>Explicator</u> 48.4 (1990): 277-80.

Colapinto, J. "Structural Family Therapy." In <u>Handbook of Family Therapy</u>, Vol. II. Eds. A.S. Gurman and D.P. Kniskern. New York: Brunner/ Mazel, 1991.

Freedman, Diane P., ed. <u>Millay at 100: A Critical Reappraisal</u>. Carbondale: S. Illinois UP, 1995.

Haley, J. <u>Problem-solving Therapy</u>. San Francisco: Jossey-Bass, 1976.

Hughes, R. and M. Perry-Jenkins. "Social Class Issues in Family Life Education." <u>Family Relations</u>, 45(2), (1996): 175-182.

Jackson, D. "Family Rules: Marital Quid Pro Quo." <u>Archives of General Psychiatry</u>, 12, (1965): 589-594.

McGoldrick, M. "Belonging and Liberation." In M. McGoldrick, Ed. <u>Re-visioning Family Therapy: Race, Culture, and Gender in Clinical Practice</u>. New York: Guilford Press, 1998.

Newcomb, John Timberman. "The Woman as Political Poet: Edna St. Vincent Millay and the Mid-Century Canon." <u>Criticism</u> 37.2 (1995): 261-77.

Nichols, M. and R. Schwartz. <u>Family Therapy: Concepts and Methods</u>. 6th ed. Boston: Allyn & Bacon, 2004.

Penn, P. "Circular Questioning." <u>Family Process</u>, 21 (1982): 267-280.

"Sonnet." <u>The New Encyclopaedia Britannica: Micropaedia</u>. 15th ed. 1993.

Thesing, William B., ed. <u>Critical Essays on Edna St. Vincent Millay</u>. New York: G.K. Hall, 1993.

Watkins, Gwen. <u>Dickens in Search of Himself: Recurrent Themes and Characters in the Work of Charles Dickens</u>. Totowa: Barnes, 1987.

Watzlawick, P., J. Beavin, and D. Jackson. <u>Pragmatics of Human Communication</u>. New York: Norton, 1967.

For internal notes and listings of Works Cited that are not represented in these or other examples throughout this book, consult your grammar/writing handbook or style manual (See Appendix H).

Walk Away Time

When the listing of Works Cited and the paper are completely drafted, give yourself permission to walk away and not think about the paper for one to three days. To be able to follow through with this step you will have to have accomplished the drafting in a timely manner, allowing yourself "paper rest" time. This step is vital. It gives you time to mentally prepare for necessary revisions that will not be apparent if you move directly from drafting to revising.

First and Second Readings

After paper rest time, pick up the paper and read it aloud completely, listening to your written thoughts. For the *first* read through, listen to your voice and to your ideas and notice when you stumble or don't understand what you are reading. These rough places are cues for revision. In the *second* read through, inspect your paper for clarity of purpose and whether or not you consistently address your specified audience. Pretend you are your audience and determine if, as a reader, you believe your needs are being addressed in every division of the paper. When you notice inconsistencies or omissions, make a note in the margin to remind yourself to come back later to make adjustments.

First Read Aloud: Writer's Perspective	**Listen for smooth flow of language**—which words need changing? **Listen for sentence development**—which sentences need to be combined, varied, simplified, expanded? **Listen to your ideas**—which ones need to be clarified, rearranged, deleted? **Listen to your tone**—does your attitude in the paper fit the topic and audience?
Second Read Aloud: Audience's Perspective	**Purpose**—is the author making the purpose obvious to me, the reader, in every major heading? **Audience**—is the author addressing my needs as a reader in every major heading? **Occasion**—as a reader, am I able to identify the reason for which this paper is being written?

ASSIGNMENTS

DRAFTING,
TRANSITIONING,
WORKS CITED,
AND READING
ALOUD

1. Drafting, transitioning, Works Cited, and reading aloud

A. Read all the information in this lesson.

B. Spend several hours drafting the remaining major headings, introduction, and conclusion, and read aloud your first finished draft.

C. Transition between introduction and first heading, between other headings, and between final heading and conclusion.

D. Properly place and format internal parenthetical notes

E. Compose the list of Works Cited.

**Drafting,
Transitioning,
Works Cited, and
Reading Aloud**

2. Collaborative learning interview: no interview this week; concentrate on the drafting and reading of your paper.

**Collaborative
Learning
Interview**

3. Evaluations: Through evaluation you identify what you already know, what you don't know at all, and what you need to learn. Making these distinctions is part of the metacognitive knowledge dimension—higher-level thinking. Realizing what you don't know is one of the prerequisites for learning.

Evaluations

A. Both you and your teacher should independently complete a *Research Evaluation Form* and an *Essay Evaluation Form*; yours is located at the end of this lesson.

B. Compare the forms to gain perspective about your experience with this part of the research learning process and with the writing process.

C. Insert the forms into the Evaluations Section of your Research Portfolio.

4. Research language: Define the following terms using the information in this lesson, in the Appendix, and in a dictionary if necessary: *transition, draft, introduction, conclusion, Works Cited, voice.* Add these terms, labeled and dated, to the Research Language section of your Research Portfolio.

**Research
Language**

5. Research portfolio: Continue organizing your three-ringed binder with its 5 major divisions—Interviews, Research Language, Evaluations, Essays, and Research Project See Appendix G).

**Research
Portfolio**

Research Evaluation Form: Student

Lesson Six

Student   _____

Date   _____

Evaluator _____

Concepts: drafting, transitioning, Works Cited, and reading aloud

	Possible Points	*Earned Points*
Concept readings completed	(10 points)	_____
Research portfolio organized and labeled	(5 points)	_____
Major headings drafted	(15 points)	_____
Introduction and conclusion drafted	(15 points)	_____
Outline detailed and finalized	(15 points)	_____
Parenthetical notes balanced with working bibliography	(10 points)	_____
Works Cited drafted	(10 points)	_____
Two read-alouds at first draft	(10 points)	_____
Student evaluation completed	(5 points)	_____
Teacher evaluation completed	(5 points)	_____

If you don't fully understand the concepts in this lesson, please review them before you move to the next step.

Student's Self-Score for *Lesson Six* _____

6. SAT Preparation Prompts

The following SAT section will help prepare you for the Scholastic Aptitude Test, a standard college entrance exam. In 2005 the SAT was revised to include additional requirements in the English field. Completing these sections in each lesson will help prepare you for this test and will also enhance your thinking and writing skills. According to *The Official SAT Study Guide for the New SAT* (99), there are three types of multiple-choice questions: identifying sentence errors, improving sentences, and improving paragraphs. Forty-nine questions on grammar and usage test your ability to use language in a consistently clear manner and to improve writing by the use of revision and editing. The multiple-choice questions don't ask you to define or use grammatical terms and don't test spelling or capitalization. Punctuation helps you know the correct answer. Because of these additions to the SAT, this curriculum includes practice with identifying sentence errors and improving sentences.

Grammar, diction, and usage equals two-thirds of your writing score on the SAT. The essay portion equals the other one-third.

Grammar, Diction, and Usage: Improving Sentences

The sentence in this section may contain an error in grammar, usage, choice of words, or idiom. Either there is just one error in the sentence or the sentence is correct. Some words or phrases are underlined and lettered; everything else in the sentence is correct.

If an underlined word or phrase is incorrect, choose that letter; if the sentence is correct, select <u>No error</u>. Then blacken the appropriate space.

1. In Spenser's *Faerie Queene* Spenser constituted specific rigid requirements for his knights and formulated a conception of earthly glory and honor which must be accompanied by virtue and service to God.

(A) In Spenser's *Faerie Queene* Spenser constituted specific rigid requirements for his knights

(B) With the knights in Spenser's *Faerie Queene* Spenser constituted specific rigid requirements for them

(C) In Spenser's, *Faerie Queene*, Spenser constituted specific rigid requirements for his knights

(D) With Spenser's knights in his *Faerie Queene* his knights underwent many specific rigid requirements

(E) In his *Faerie Queene* Spenser constituted specific rigid requirements for his knights

(A)　(B)　(C)　(D)　(E)

2. Common in the works of both Calderón and Spenser, were the virtues of obedience, fealty, adoration, and self-sacrifice, in addition to the direct regard of honor and chivalry.

(A) Common in the works of both Calderón and Spenser,

(B) However common in the works of both Calderón and Spenser,

(C) Common in the works of both Calderón and Spenser, however,

(D) Common in the works of both Calderón and Spenser, however;

(E) However; common in the works of both Calderón and Spenser

(A)　(B)　(C)　(D)　(E)

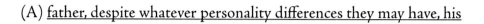

3. It was assumed by his family and social class that Charles would grow up to be exactly like his <u>father, despite whatever personality differences they may have, his</u> needs to search for his own identity are not considered.

(A) <u>father, despite whatever personality differences they may have, his</u>

(B) father; despite whatever personality differences they may have his

(C) father, despite whatever personality differences they may have; his

(D) father, despite whatever personality differences they may have, his

(E) father, despite whatever personality differences they may have. His

(A)   (B)   (C)   (D)   (E)

4. <u>The capitals architecture and dynastys name</u> alone never could have unified Khubilai's empire.

(A) <u>The capitals architecture and dynastys name</u>

(B) The capitals' architecture and dynastys' name

(C) The capital's architecture and dynasty's name

(D) The capital architecture and dynasty name

(E) The capital's architecture and dynastys' name

(A)   (B)   (C)   (D)   (E)

**SAT
Essay
Writing**

7. SAT Essay Writing

The SAT "assesses your ability to develop and express ideas effectively; [it] evaluate[s] your ability to do the kind of writing required in college—writing that develops a point of view, presents ideas logically and clearly, and uses precise language . . . [the essay is] written in a limited time, which doesn't allow for many revisions, so it is considered and scored as a first draft" (Official 99).

Use this curriculum to prepare for the revised edition of the SAT, which includes writing and grammar elements in addition to three critical reading sections. Use the following pages dedicated to essay writing; they will help you organize and write your thoughts into essay format. Evaluation forms follow: one for you, and one for the sample SAT essay.

Successful writing includes:

1. A clearly expressed thesis statement

2. Well-developed ideas with relevant and accurate supporting information

3. Good organization

4. Appropriate, accurate, and varied vocabulary

5. Variety of sentence structure (syntax)

(Official 106)

The SAT allows you 46 lines on which to write between 300 and 400 words in a persuasive essay. It is important to write legibly because graders will spend approximately one to two minutes reading your essay. They will not spend time trying to decipher your handwriting. Use your two pages wisely, not writing in large letters or leaving extra wide margins. Your goal is to persuade your reader of your position.

**Planning
Essay Six**

Allot three to five minutes to think about and plan the essay—completing the statement. Understand the statements and take a position.

In two pages write about your position on one of the following statements; you have *no more than twenty-five minutes.*

Complete the statement

> *Communicating with an audience requires a basic understanding*
> *of who comprises the audience. A good example of effective communication*
> *with an audience is* _____.

Assignment: Complete the sentence above with a fictional work from literature, film, or television and write a persuasive essay demonstrating how that story taught an important truth.

Initial thoughts about this statement:

_____

_____

Do I agree or disagree with this statement?

_____

_____

Reasons/support/evidence for my position (why I maintain this position):

I. Example from history, literature, popular culture, current events, or personal experience:

_____

_____

II. Example from history, literature, popular culture, current events, or personal experience:

_____

_____

III. Example from history, literature, popular culture, current events, or personal experience:

_____

_____

These thoughts become the outline for your essay. Do not take more than three to five minutes to organize these thoughts. These first *three to five minutes are crucial to the thinking skills* you will exhibit in the essay.

You will need the *next twenty minutes to persuade your audience* of your position on the issue, to support your position as you move from idea to idea, and to use appropriate vocabulary and varied sentence structure free from grammar, mechanics, and usage errors.

It is important not to change your position in the middle of the essay because you won't have time to rework the essay.

You are now ready to write the essay on two sheets of paper. Your goal is to write between 300 and 400 words on the issue.

It is very important to *time the writing*.

Communicating with an Audience
Essay Six

Your Title:

_____

_____

_____

_____

_____

_____

_____

_____

_____

_____

_____

_____

_____

_____

_____

_____

_____

_____

_____

_____

_____

Evaluate your essay using the following criteria as a guide; a scoring section follows this chart.

PRACTICE ESSAY
EVALUATION
FORM:
STUDENT

Lesson Six

Level 6	Level 5	Level 4	Level 3	Level 2	Level 1
Insightful - Outstanding	**Effective - Solid**	**Competent - Adequate**	**Inadequate - Limited**	**Seriously flawed**	**Deficient**
Convincing development of a position on the issue	Proficient, coherent development of a position on the issue	Workmanlike development of a position on the issue	Sketchy development of a position on the issue	Limited development of a position on the issue	Lack of a position on the issue
Selection of relevant examples and evidence to support writer's position	Selection of basically relevant evidence to support writer's position	Selection of reasonably appropriate evidence to support writer's position	Selection of weak or inappropriate evidence to support writer's position	Selection of weak or inappropriate evidence to support writer's position	Absence of evidence to support a point of view
Smooth, well-orchestrated progression from idea to idea	Relatively well-ordered progression from idea to idea	Acceptable progression from idea to idea	Erratic progression from idea to idea	Tendency toward incoherence	Absence of focus and organization
Use of varied sentence types and appropriate vocabulary	Reasonably varied sentence structure and reasonable vocabulary	Somewhat varied sentence structure and somewhat varied vocabulary	Somewhat limited vocabulary and inadequately varied sentence structure	Highly limited vocabulary and numerous problems with sentence structure	Rudimentary vocabulary and severe problems with sentence structure
Freedom from most technical flaws (grammar, usage, diction)	Relative freedom from technical flaws	Some flaws in mechanics, usage, and grammar	Multiple flaws in mechanics, usage, and grammar	Errors in mechanics, usage, and grammar serious enough to interfere with the reader's comprehension	Extensive flaws in mechanics, usage, and grammar severe enough to block the reader's comprehension

(Barron's 301, Kaplan 21, Official 105)

Level 6: demonstrates a clear command of writing and thinking skills despite the occasional, infrequent minor error.
Level 5: exhibits a generally dependable command of writing and thinking skills despite some mistakes.
Level 4: exhibits a generally adequate command of writing and thinking skills although the skills are typically inconsistent in quality.
Level 3: exhibits an insufficient command of writing and thinking skills although the skills show some signs of developing proficiency.
Level 2: exhibits a quite flawed command of writing and thinking skills.
Level 1: exhibits an acutely flawed command of writing and thinking skills.

Student's self-score of essay (between 1 and 6) _____

**Sample
Student
Essay**

Read the following essay and then determine the score you would give it based on the scoring criteria and word count. Using moral and religious arguments and references, this student responded (in over 500 words) to the following SAT Essay prompt

Respond to the following statement:

Worldwide themes of the existence of good and evil are debated in many venues of life.

<u>Assignment</u>: The statement above implies that both good and evil really exist. Do you agree or disagree? Write a persuasive essay supporting, disputing, or qualifying the statement. You may use examples from history, literature, popular culture, current events, or personal experience to support your position.

Evil is there All Right

The first Buddha taught that suffering and evil were a matter of perspective. People grieve over what they call "evil" because they desire the opposite: good, ease, and pleasure. Evil, which does not exist as an actual force, disappears with a perspective change. Evil does exist as a powerful force for dualists, though. They explain life as a gigantic interplay between the equal forces of good and evil, or light and dark. When good wins a battle, life is enjoyable; just as often, though, situations turn difficult when it is evil's turn to influence the world. The best approach to dealing with undesirable events is just to expect them. They always come and they always go.

Some Christians recommend a perspective change similar to Buddha's for people discontent with the unfairness of their circumstances. They assure struggling people that since God controls everything, He wills painful situations because nothing could happen contrary to God's deliberate intentions. Heartless religious folk try to convince people broken by suffering that evil is actually good for them. Something considered bad actually saves someone from something else much worse that could have happened. According to this thinking, coming to terms with evil involves deadening the outrage that God would allow it and becoming convinced that the long-term good it causes outweighs the initial pain.

These attempts to resolve the problem of evil deny the intensity of the human experience of evil. Buddhism faults humans for their grief, because it is their attachment to the experiential world that allows a sensation or idea of pain. Dualism stifles extreme anger, pain, or sadness over good's opposite. Perhaps worst of all are the pseudo-Christian excuses about evil being caused, enhancing the appreciation of good, warding off even more atrocious things, and effecting positive growth.

Atheists decry the assertion that God exists not only because the statement cannot be verified but also because the existence of evil in the world seems to contradict the theistic notion of a sovereign, benevolent God. They either atheistically dismiss God's existence, believe that God is actually sadistic, or conclude as did Rabbi Kushner that God is unable to stop evil.

Orthodox Christianity succeeds without contradicting itself in recognizing evil and in believing in an all-good, almighty God. By creating humans as finite beings, God did not steel His creation off from sickness, physical weakness, and death; in other words, evil does not threaten God's position of all-powerful Creator. Because God gave His human creatures the ability to choose good or evil, He cannot be blamed for their choices to injure one another—He remains all-good.

Christianity is supremely advantageous over Buddhism, dualism, and other weak resolutions of evil in the way it values the intensity of human experience of evil: God Himself became a human and experienced evil. The human/God suffered intensely but did not cause any evil to others. People who believe in Jesus' historical existence and in His evil-defying salvation are called the Church, a metaphor for His physical body. God is present with His Church through His Holy Spirit. God created the world, lived and died and returned to life in it, and remains in it.

Orthodox Christianity manages to hold in one hand both the blatant misery and unfairness so prevalent on the earth and the uncompromisable goodness of the omnipotent God. It does not discount human experience or excuse humanity's furthering of evil in its provision of a hope for future redemption. Jesus enables the Church to pay even greater attention to evil than does the social critique and to counteract evil with good. _____

_____

_____

_____

Evaluate the student's essay using the following criteria as a guide; a scoring section follows this chart.

SAMPLE ESSAY EVALUATION FORM

Lesson Six

Level 6	Level 5	Level 4	Level 3	Level 2	Level 1
Insightful - Outstanding	Effective - Solid	Competent - Adequate	Inadequate - Limited	Seriously flawed	Deficient
Convincing development of a position on the issue	Proficient, coherent development of a position on the issue	Workmanlike development of a position on the issue	Sketchy development of a position on the issue	Limited development of a position on the issue	Lack of a position on the issue
Selection of relevant examples and evidence to support writer's position	Selection of basically relevant evidence to support writer's position	Selection of reasonably appropriate evidence to support writer's position	Selection of weak or inappropriate evidence to support writer's position	Selection of weak or inappropriate evidence to support writer's position	Absence of evidence to support a point of view
Smooth, well-orchestrated progression from idea to idea	Relatively well-ordered progression from idea to idea	Acceptable progression from idea to idea	Erratic progression from idea to idea	Tendency toward incoherence	Absence of focus and organization
Use of varied sentence types and appropriate vocabulary	Reasonably varied sentence structure and reasonable vocabulary	Somewhat varied sentence structure and somewhat varied vocabulary	Somewhat limited vocabulary and inadequately varied sentence structure	Highly limited vocabulary and numerous problems with sentence structure	Rudimentary vocabulary and severe problems with sentence structure
Freedom from most technical flaws (grammar, usage, diction)	Relative freedom from technical flaws	Some flaws in mechanics, usage, and grammar	Multiple flaws in mechanics, usage, and grammar	Errors in mechanics, usage, and grammar serious enough to interfere with the reader's comprehension	Extensive flaws in mechanics, usage, and grammar severe enough to block the reader's comprehension

(Barron's 301, Kaplan 21, Official 105)

Level 6: demonstrates a clear command of writing and thinking skills despite the occasional, infrequent minor error.
Level 5: exhibits a generally dependable command of writing and thinking skills despite some mistakes.
Level 4: exhibits a generally adequate command of writing and thinking skills although the skills are typically inconsistent in quality.
Level 3: exhibits an insufficient command of writing and thinking skills although the skills show some signs of developing proficiency.
Level 2: exhibits a quite flawed command of writing and thinking skills.
Level 1: exhibits an acutely flawed command of writing and thinking skills.

Student's self-score of essay (between 1 and 6) _____

[Based on criteria and assignment length, the SAT evaluator's score for this essay is 6].

LESSON SEVEN

FORMATTING, REVISING, EDITING, AND PEER REVIEWING

A. Concepts

**Lesson Seven
Overview**

1. Formatting

2. Revising

3. Editing

4. Peer reviewing

B. Assignments

1. Collaborative learning interview: peer reviewer

2. Research language: *format, print, revise, edit, effective sentences, paragraph, grammar, diction, punctuation, mechanics*

3. Research portfolio

4. Evaluations

5. SAT prep prompts: grammar, diction, and usage—improving sentences; essay writing

6. Sample essay

CONCEPTS

Formatting,
Revising,
Editing,
and Peer
Reviewing

Formatting the Research Paper

You have passed through critical points of the research process. In Lesson Six you drafted the paper, including the introduction, conclusion, and the Works Cited; you transitioned between headings and subheadings; and you read the paper aloud to listen for smooth flow of language, for sentence development, and to assess your ideas, your purpose, and your faithfulness to your audience. It is now time to consider proper formatting. You may be associated with a school or business that allows research to be written long hand with pen and paper. If so, use regular lined paper abiding by its left margin and writing on one side of the paper only. Do not double-space hand-written papers. Most schools and businesses in North America expect computer generated work. If you already have appropriate computer skills, you are ready to format your drafted paper. If you lack the necessary computer skills, consider asking a friend for help or taking a computer class to gain these skills. This lesson is devoted to proper formatting, revising the drafted paper, editing the drafted paper, and printing the draft.

Paper

Formal writing requires standard white, good quality paper that measures 8½ by 11 inches. High school research papers are not expected to meet the requirements that college research papers, theses, and dissertations meet (20-pound bond paper). If you are unable to type your paper and your instructor will accept a hand-written paper, use regular notebook paper.

Margins

Allow one inch on all sides of the paper for margins. Page numbers will invade the margin in the upper right corner. Occasionally, instructors prefer a 1½ inch left-side margin if they require a special binding. Indent paragraphs one-half inch from the left margin and indent long quotations one inch from the left margin. Do not justify the lines of your paper to make the right side margin even. If you are handwriting on notebook paper, write only on one side of the paper; use the margin lines that are on the paper, leaving a one-inch margin at the bottom; and write in dark blue or black ink.

Pagination

Page numbers are placed in the upper right corner one-half inch from the top and flush with the right margin. Position your last name before the page number on every page in case pages get lost or rearranged. For example: Moss 162 in the margin of the upper right hand corner indicates that Moss authored this paper and that this is page 162. Computers make this process simple since they do the work for you after you type in the initial setting. Note that there is no abbreviation, no parentheses, and no period with the page number. Throughout the manuscript, number all pages consecutively. Begin page numbers on the first page of the paper, even if your instructor requires a cover page.

Spacing

Double space research papers throughout, including heading, endnotes, and the Works Cited. This arrangement accommodates reading and gives your instructor ample room to comment on the paper.

Heading and Title

Begin the heading one inch from the top at the left margin on the first page. Type your name on the first line, your instructor's name on the second line, the course name on the third line, and the date on the fourth line, double spacing between each line. Double space again and center your title on the next line. Double space between the title and the first line of the paper, which you will indent to signify the first paragraph of your paper. Follow standard capitalization rules for your title and do not underline it, italicize it, or put it in quotation marks (unless your title contains the title of another work that requires such punctuation). Having an effective title is your reader's first guide to your paper. Make it appropriate and precise.

Example One: Pagination, Heading, Title, and Introductory Paragraph

1"

Sheila E. Moss   Moss 1

Dr. T. Coy Porter

British Literature

April 12, 2005

Some Influences of the Arthurian Legends on English and Spanish Literature

Was Arthur a man or merely a myth? Scholarly attitudes vary so

greatly that arriving at a definite conclusion is difficult. However, so that

the facts and fancies of both opinions may be examined, the statements of

recognized Arthurian scholars will present the views between the historical   1"

Arthur and the mythical Arthur.

Example Two: Pagination, Heading, Title, and Introductory Paragraph

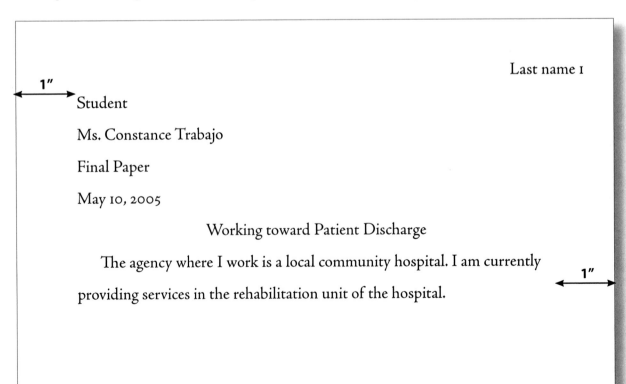

Last name 1

1"

Student

Ms. Constance Trabajo

Final Paper

May 10, 2005

Working toward Patient Discharge

The agency where I work is a local community hospital. I am currently   1"

providing services in the rehabilitation unit of the hospital.

Example Three: Pagination, Heading, Title, and Introductory Paragraph

1"

Last name 1

Student

Mr. D.J. Sloan

American Literature

February, 2006

Some Subjects Addressed in Edna St. Vincent Millay's Sonnets

Many critics agree that Edna St. Vincent Millay's sonnets are

her best literary works. She writes in the traditional Petrarchan or

Shakespearean forms, with either an octet/sestet or a triple-quatrain/

couplet pattern ("Sonnet" 13). Millay's various literary influences obviously

1"

affect her choice to pursue sonnet writing, though she approaches the

sonnet with uncustomary female perspectives. She incorporates her

viewpoints into sonnets centered around politics, time, and love.

Tables and Illustrations

High school research may not contain tables and illustrations, but if you need to include them, they should be placed as close as possible to the text they relate to. Identify tables and illustrations with the words Table or Illustration, an Arabic numeral, and a caption. Type the label and the caption flush left above the table or the illustration and capitalize them using typical capitalization rules for titles—not all caps.

Print

Do not justify the lines of your paper. Typically, lines justified by computers add spaces between words or letters, and that can irritate readers. Justifying lines also complicates end of line breaks. Use a standard font type and size, for example Times New Roman 12 point, Courier 12 point, or Arial 12 point. Occasionally, your instructor will allow 10 point font for notes or even the paper. Unless directed otherwise, keep the same font style and size throughout the paper.

Allow yourself plenty of time to experiment with margins, spacing, pagination, and printing since difficulty with these issues can cause you to miss your deadline.

Unless your educator gives you different instructions, research papers are typically submitted without a binder and are held together with a paper clip, or stapled in the upper left corner.

Revising the Research Paper

Revising (looking again at), editing, and proofreading are three very important parts of writing research, and it is important to know the difference between them. This lesson deals with revising and editing, and Lesson Eight deals with proofreading. Editing usually follows revising, but many writers constantly revise and edit as they write. As long as you don't get bogged down to the point of losing your writing momentum and thus your thoughts, it's all right to both revise and edit as you write. However, some writers do better work if they write freely without revising and editing until they have produced a first draft. Nevertheless, some revising is inherent in the research process, and you've already been doing a good deal of it. As you planned and researched, you constantly reorganized, rearranged, added, and deleted. That is a form of process revision. In Lesson Six you were asked to draft your paper and then to read it aloud twice.

Reading your paper aloud was the beginning of content revision. Now you are ready to continue revising and incorporating the results of the read aloud into the paper. Those places where you stumbled in the reading or wondered what you were talking about are the first places to consider revising. Why did you stumble? Do you need a different word? A different arrangement of words? Do you need to move a paragraph to another place? Delete a paragraph? Delete a sentence? Add more information in order to clarify the point you were trying to make? Discover why the place seemed awkward and why it doesn't make sense. Ask yourself, "What else does my reader need to know here? How can I help the reader better understand what I mean to say?"

This stage of revision addresses the content of your paper. The read alouds give you a big picture, or global, look at your paper. Print off a copy and take a long look at what you have produced. Use the following checkpoints to revise the paper as a whole.

Global Revision of Content Checklist Points

Page numbers needing revision

_____	Do I adhere to my thesis throughout the paper?
_____	Have I collated my paper with my final outline?
_____	Is there a smooth flow of language throughout the paper? Where are the rough spots?
_____	Have I evaluated paragraphs for their main ideas and development?
_____	Do I have extraneous information that needs to be deleted?
_____	Have I rearranged sentences or paragraphs if they fit better in another place?
_____	Is each paragraph coherent?
_____	Which ideas in my paragraphs need to be clarified, rearranged, or deleted?
_____	Have I used transition elements between paragraphs and major headings?
_____	Is the purpose for which I'm writing this paper obvious in every major heading?
_____	Does my paper fit the occasion for which I am writing it? (Occasion may be defined as the context in which the writing occurs—the time, place, and specifics for the research—and may center on your response to events in the world, a specific paper written at the request of an instructor, the expectation of the research, the scope of the research, the deadline for the research, or any element that affects the writing of the research.)
_____	Does my tone in the paper appropriately express my attitude toward the topic and the audience and the occasion for which I'm writing?
_____	Does my introduction present a clear thesis and a "hook" for my audience?
_____	Is my conclusion appropriate for the purpose of my paper, and will it satisfy the expectation of my audience?
_____	Do I fully address the needs of my readers in every major heading—am I making sense to the reader?
_____	Is there something missing that my reader will need to know? Have I corrected these problems?

Using these checkpoints can facilitate the revision process and direct you to specific corrections. Make those revisions now before advancing to editing. Repeat these steps until you are satisfied that all elements are properly in place.

Editing the Research Paper

Some elements of revising and editing overlap. Just as you constantly revise throughout the writing process, so do you edit. However, the edit that comes after global revision is far more precise and challenging. If you enjoy a challenge, consider revision and editing as a hunting game: it is your opportunity to find all those elements that cause difficulty in your writing. Find them *before* your instructor does. Remember, the more problems you find and solve, the fewer the instructor will find!

Detailed Editing Checkpoints

Grammar and sentence structure: as you read through your computer draft on-screen and then through your printed draft, identify problems and record the page number.

Pages for revision

_____ Fragments
_____ Adjectives and adverbs
_____ Pronouns and antecedents
_____ Sentence unity: consistency
_____ Parallelism
_____ Have I corrected sentences that need to be combined, varied, simplified, or expanded?

Pages for revision

_____ Comma splices and fused sentences
_____ Verb and subject agreement; tense and person shift
_____ Misplaced parts and dangling modifiers
_____ Subordination and coordination
_____ Emphasis

Diction

Pages for revision

_____ Usage

_____ Exactness
_____ Have I corrected sentences with diction problems?

Pages for revision

_____ Conciseness—avoiding wordiness and needless repetition
_____ Clarity and Completeness

Punctuation and Mechanics

Pages for revision   *Pages for revision*

_____   Comma   _____   Semicolon
_____   Apostrophe   _____   Periods, en and em dashes, and question marks
_____   Quotation marks
_____   Have I corrected sentences with punctuation and mechanics problems?

Spelling and Hyphenation

Pages for revision   *Pages for revision*

_____   Capitals   _____   Italics
_____   Abbreviations and numbers   _____   Misspelled words
_____   Have I corrected sentences with spelling and hyphenation problems? (Note: do not rely solely on computer promptings for finding errors; computers will not differentiate between such usage errors as *their* for *there* or *in* for *if*, etc.)

Manuscript documentation

Pages for revision   *Pages for revision*

_____   Parenthetical notes   _____   Works Cited

Peer Review of the Paper

After you correct these rough places in your paper, print a copy of the paper for a peer to read. Ask the peer to consult the Global Revision and Detailed Editing Checkpoints. Then, ask the peer to read your paper aloud to you. Encourage your peer reviewer to really help you identify problem spots. Invite your peer to be honest about the paper in a spirit of being helpful without harshness. Another set of eyes can find troublesome spots that your eyes have skipped because you are so familiar with the subject by now. If both of you are writing research, peer reviewing can be a mutually beneficial arrangement as you swap paper reviews.

Without being defensive about your work, try to really hear what the peer reviewer tells you. You have worked so closely with your paper for so long that you are no longer as objective as the peer can be. When there is a question, give serious attention to whether or not that part of the paper needs more revision. In the final analysis, however, it is your paper, and you will make the decision about the reviewer's suggestions and comments.

1. **Formatting, revising, editing, and peer reviewing**

ASSIGNMENTS

Lesson
Seven

181

FORMATTING,
REVISING,
EDITING, AND
PEER REVIEWING

   A. **Read** all the information in this lesson.

   B. **Spend several hours** formatting, revising, editing, and inviting a peer review of your paper according to the following lists:

   Formatting the research paper

Formatting

   Paper

   Margins

   Pagination

   Spacing

   Heading and title

   Tables and illustrations

   Print

   Revising the research paper: checkpoints for global revision

Revising

   Thesis

   Paragraphing

   Purpose

   Audience

   Occasion

   Outline

   Transitions

   Editing the research paper: checkpoints for detailed editing

Editing

   Grammar and sentence structure

   Diction

   Punctuation and mechanics

   Spelling and hyphenation

   Parenthetical notes and Works Cited

   Peer revision of the research paper:

**Peer
Reviewing**

   Global Revision and Detailed Editing Checkpoints

2. **Collaborative learning interview** with a peer reviewer. Enter into a collaborative learning experience by arranging for a read-through interview with your peer reviewer; plan questions for the interview; take notes during the

**Collaborative
Learning
Interview**

interview; organize the notes. The purpose of this interview is to hear the opinion of your peer reviewer regarding your printed draft of research. sListen carefully to specifics.

> **Step A:** Call or personally arrange for a 30-45 minute meeting with your peer reviewer. Courteously state your reasons for requesting the review: you are finalizing your research project and are interested in the peer's perspectives on the progress of your paper.

> **Step B:** Copy the Global Revision and Detailed Editing Checkpoints for the peer reviewer.

> **Step C:** Use the Global Revision and Detailed Editing Checkpoints from the peer reviewer to guide your interview. Take notes on what the reviewer tells you. Be respectful, sensitive, and courteous. You are taking valuable time which is being granted to you.

> **Step D:** Organize your peer review; use the results of this review to help with final revisions and edits.

Evaluations

3. **Evaluations:** Through evaluation you identify what you already know, what you don't know at all, and what you need to learn. Making these distinctions is part of the metacognitive knowledge dimension—higher-level thinking. Realizing what you don't know is one of the prerequisites for learning.

> **A.** Both you and your teacher should independently complete a *Research Evaluation Form* and an *Essay Evaluation Form*; yours is located at the end of this lesson.

> **B.** Compare the forms to gain perspective about your experience with this part of the research learning process and with the writing process.

> **C.** Insert the forms into the Evaluations Section of your Research Portfolio.

**Research
Language**

4. **Research language:** Define the following terms as they relate to researched writing, using the information in this lesson, in the Appendix, and in a dictionary if necessary: *format, print, revise, edit, effective sentences, paragraph, grammar, diction, punctuation, mechanics.* Add these terms, labeled and dated, to the Research Language section of your Research Portfolio.

**Research
Portfolio**

5. **Research portfolio:** Continue organizing your three-ringed binder with its 5 m divisions—Interviews, Research Language, Evaluations, Essays, and Research Project (See Appendix G).

RESEARCH
EVALUATION
FORM:
STUDENT

Lesson Seven

Student _____

Date _____

Evaluator _____

Concepts: formatting, revising, editing, and peer reviewing

	Possible Points	*Earned Points*
Concept readings completed	(20 points)	_____
Research portfolio organized and labeled	(5 points)	_____
First printing (formatting)	(20 points)	_____
First revision checkpoints (thesis, outline, purpose, audience, transitions)	(20 points)	_____
First edit checkpoints (effective sentences, paragraphing, grammar, diction, punctuation, mechanics, parenthetical notes, Works Cited)	(20 points)	_____
Interview with peer reviewer completed	(5 points)	_____
Student evaluation completed	(5 points)	_____
Teacher evaluation completed	(5 points)	_____

If you don't fully understand the concepts in this lesson, please review them before you move to the next step.

Student's Self-Score for *Lesson Seven* _____

SAT Preparation Prompts

6. SAT Preparation Prompts

The following SAT section will help prepare you for the Scholastic Aptitude Test, a standard college entrance exam. In 2005 the SAT was revised to include additional requirements in the English field. Completing these sections in each lesson will help prepare you for this test and will also enhance your thinking and writing skills. According to *The Official SAT Study Guide for the New SAT* (99), there are three types of multiple-choice questions: identifying sentence errors, improving sentences, and improving paragraphs. Forty-nine questions on grammar and usage test your ability to use language in a consistently clear manner and to improve writing by the use of revision and editing. The multiple-choice questions don't ask you to define or use grammatical terms and don't test spelling or capitalization. Punctuation helps you know the correct answer. Because of these additions to the SAT, this curriculum includes practice with identifying sentence errors and improving sentences.

Grammar, diction, and usage equals two-thirds of your writing score on the SAT. The essay portion equals the other one-third.

Grammar, Diction, and Usage: Improving Sentences

Some or all parts of the following sentences are underlined. The first answer choice, (A), simply repeats the underlined part of the sentence. The other four choices present four alternative ways to phrase the underlined part. Select the answer that produces the most effective sentence, one that is clear and exact, and blacken the appropriate space. In selecting your choice, be sure that it is standard written English, and that it expresses the meaning of the original sentence.

1. <u>Spenser's gentleman was careful of his own conduct but Calderón's gentleman</u> guarded his family's conduct even more closely in order to insure his own honor.

(A) <u>Spenser's gentleman was careful of his own conduct but Calderón's gentleman</u>

(B) Spenser's gentleman was careful of his own conduct, and Calderón's gentleman

(C) While Spenser's gentleman was careful of his own conduct, Calderón's gentleman

(D) Spenser's gentleman but not Calderón's gentleman was careful of his own conduct and Calderón's gentleman

(E) Both the gentlemen in Spenser's and Calderón's conduct

(A)   (B)   (C)   (D)   (E)

2. <u>Neither the culture, the theater, or the literature</u> would tolerate the slightest break with the code of honor.

(A) <u>Neither the culture, the theater, or the literature</u>

(B) Not even the culture or the theater nor the literature

(C) Not the culture, the theater, not even the literature

(D) Neither the culture, the theater, and not the literature

(E) Neither the culture, the theater, nor the literature

(A)   (B)   (C)   (D)   (E)

3. "The code of honor has been handed down to you and I by way of standards of courtesy, manners, and general socialization," explains Professor Porter.

(A) "The code of honor has been handed down to you and I by way of standards of courtesy, manners, and general socialization," explains

(B) "The code of honor has been handed down to you and I, by way of standards of courtesy, manners, and general socialization," explains

(C) "The code of honor has been handed down to you and I; by way of standards of courtesy, manners, and general socialization,"

(D) "The code of honor has been handed down to you and me by way of standards of courtesy, manners, and general socialization," explains

(E) "The code of honor has been handed down to you and I by way of standards of courtesy, manners, and general socialization." explains

(A)   (B)   (C)   (D)   (E)

4. How could Dickens have such intimate insight into a child's pain accept through personal experience?

(A) insight into a child's pain accept through personal experience?

(B) insight into a childs' pain accept through personal experience?

(C) insight into a child's pain; except through personal experience?

(D) insight into a child's pain except through personal experience?

(E) insight into a child's pain, accept through personal experience?

(A)   (B)   (C)   (D)   (E)

7. SAT Essay Writing

The SAT "assesses your ability to develop and express ideas effectively; [it] evaluate[s] your ability to do the kind of writing required in college—writing that develops a point of view, presents ideas logically and clearly, and uses precise language . . . [the essay is] written in a limited time, which doesn't allow for many revisions, so it is considered and scored as a first draft" (Official 99).

Use this curriculum to prepare for the revised edition of the SAT, which includes writing and grammar elements in addition to three critical reading sections. Use the following pages dedicated to essay writing; they will help you organize and write your thoughts into essay format. Evaluation forms follow: one for you, and one for the sample SAT essay.

Successful writing includes:

1. A clearly expressed thesis statement

2. Well-developed ideas with relevant and accurate supporting information

3. Good organization

4. Appropriate, accurate, and varied vocabulary

5. Variety of sentence structure (syntax)

(Official 106)

The SAT allows you 46 lines on which to write between 300 and 400 words in a persuasive essay. It is important to write legibly because graders will spend approximately one to two minutes reading your essay. They will not spend time trying to decipher your handwriting. Use your two pages wisely, not writing in large letters or leaving extra wide margins. Your goal is to persuade your reader of your position.

Allot three to five minutes to think about and plan the essay. Make sure you understand the statement and then take a position.

**Planning
Essay Seven**

Write about the following statement in two pages; you have *no more than twenty-five minutes.*

Allot three to five minutes to think about the issue for this essay. Respond to the statement:

Smooth transitions in writing illustrate the benefits of smooth transitions in life.

Assignment: The statement above implies that smooth transitions are optimal in both writing and life. Write an essay supporting, disputing, or qualifying the statement. You may use examples from history, literature, popular culture, current events, or personal experience to support your position.

Which statement do I most agree with?

_____

_____

Reasons/support/evidence for my position (why I agree with it):

I. Example from history, literature, popular culture, current events, or personal experience:

_____

_____

II. Example from history, literature, popular culture, current events, or personal experience:

_____

_____

III. Example from history, literature, popular culture, current events, or personal experience:

_____

_____

These thoughts become the outline for your essay. Do not take more than three to five minutes to organize these thoughts. These first *three to five minutes are crucial to the thinking skills* you will exhibit in the essay.

You will need the *next twenty minutes to persuade your audience* of your position on the issue, to support your position as you move from idea to idea, and to use appropriate vocabulary and varied sentence structure free from grammar, mechanics, and usage errors.

It is important not to change your position in the middle of the essay because you won't have time to rework the essay.

You are now ready to write the essay on two sheets of paper. Your goal is to write between 300 and 400 words on the issue.

It is very important to *time the writing*.

Smooth Transitions
Essay Seven

Your Title: _____

_____

_____

_____

_____

_____

_____

_____

_____

_____

_____

_____

_____

_____

_____

_____

_____

_____

_____

_____

_____

_____

_____

_____

_____

_____

_____

_____

_____

_____

_____

_____

_____

_____

_____

_____

_____

_____

_____

_____

_____

_____

_____

_____

_____

_____

_____

_____

_____

_____

PRACTICE ESSAY
EVALUATION
FORM:
STUDENT

Lesson Seven

Evaluate your essay using the following criteria as a guide; a scoring section follows this chart.

Level 6	Level 5	Level 4	Level 3	Level 2	Level 1
Insightful - Outstanding	Effective - Solid	Competent - Adequate	Inadequate - Limited	Seriously flawed	Deficient
Convincing development of a position on the issue	Proficient, coherent development of a position on the issue	Workmanlike development of a position on the issue	Sketchy development of a position on the issue	Limited development of a position on the issue	Lack of a position on the issue
Selection of relevant examples and evidence to support writer's position	Selection of basically relevant evidence to support writer's position	Selection of reasonably appropriate evidence to support writer's position	Selection of weak or inappropriate evidence to support writer's position	Selection of weak or inappropriate evidence to support writer's position	Absence of evidence to support a point of view
Smooth, well-orchestrated progression from idea to idea	Relatively well-ordered progression from idea to idea	Acceptable progression from idea to idea	Erratic progression from idea to idea	Tendency toward incoherence	Absence of focus and organization
Use of varied sentence types and appropriate vocabulary	Reasonably varied sentence structure and reasonable vocabulary	Somewhat varied sentence structure and somewhat varied vocabulary	Somewhat limited vocabulary and inadequately varied sentence structure	Highly limited vocabulary and numerous problems with sentence structure	Rudimentary vocabulary and severe problems with sentence structure
Freedom from most technical flaws (grammar, usage, diction)	Relative freedom from technical flaws	Some flaws in mechanics, usage, and grammar	Multiple flaws in mechanics, usage, and grammar	Errors in mechanics, usage, and grammar serious enough to interfere with the reader's comprehension	Extensive flaws in mechanics, usage, and grammar severe enough to block the reader's comprehension

(Barron's 301, Kaplan 21, Official 105)

Level 6: demonstrates a clear command of writing and thinking skills despite the occasional, infrequent minor error.

Level 5: exhibits a generally dependable command of writing and thinking skills despite some mistakes.

Level 4: exhibits a generally adequate command of writing and thinking skills although the skills are typically inconsistent in quality.

Level 3: exhibits an insufficient command of writing and thinking skills although the skills show some signs of developing proficiency.

Level 2: exhibits a quite flawed command of writing and thinking skills.

Level 1: exhibits an acutely flawed command of writing and thinking skills.

Student's self-score of essay (between 1 and 6) _____

Sample
Student
Essay

Lesson
Seven

193

Read the following essay and then determine the score you would give it based on the scoring criteria and word count. Using literary allusions and references, this student responds (in 475 words) to the following SAT Essay prompt.

Respond to the following statement:

The idea of character has been introduced into society through various means. One of those means is through _____.

Assignment: Consider the statement above. Decide on a position that represents your beliefs and write a persuasive essay explaining your position. You may use examples from history, literature, popular culture, current events, or personal experience to support your position.

Flannery O'Connor's Way

Flannery O'Connor's use of grotesque situations and violence destroys illusions held by the characters in her stories. For all her manipulation, rudeness, and arrogance in being a "lady," the grandmother has no verbal or mental control over the Misfit in "A Good Man is Hard to Find." The criminal's gun and his resistance to religious platitudes exhaust the grandmother's store of control methods, and she ends up sitting in her own blood. Just before being shot, however, the grandmother has a moment of genuine compassion for the convict. His violent reaction steeply contrasts her tenderness. While the Misfit repays genuine grace with violence, the boys in "A Circle in the Fire" retaliate against false kindness. As they see through Mrs. Cope's feigned hospitality, they grow less and less respectful of her property.

Their misdemeanors eventually lead to full-fledged, premeditated arson. Their violence shoots down Mrs. Cope's appearance of kindness and concern. Mrs. Cope's morbid friend Mrs. Pritchard thrives on violence and gruesomeness. Mrs. Cope avoids it or "copes" with it by forced gratitude; by reminding God how much he has given her, she warns him not to take it from her. When the boys burn her woods, they expose her shallow trust in God. O'Connor's characters illustrate various traits of "character" that trickle down to society through literature.

O'Connor's improper or impolite content matter often serves to contrast the way her characters act with the way they pretend to act. Red Sammy's flapping beer gut proves him an uncultured, backwoods hick instead of the controlled, proper gentleman his speech sets him up to be. Other times, the distasteful descriptions force readers to accept the negative aspects of her characters. The infuriatingly bratty John Wesley and June Star seem pitiful and innocent as they are about to be shot. Earlier in the story, though, they are clearly disrespectful, selfish, pompous snobs. O'Connor realistically portrays them as self-interested children. The girl in "A Circle in the Fire" even charges into the woods with two pistols, seeking the equally un-innocent boys who vandalize her home. Unpleasant content matter also requires the reader to believe the tragedy of the situation. The author describes the pool of blood in which the grandmother of "A Good Man . . ." dies. She observes the grandmother's posture and facial expression. The description is morbid but demands that readers acknowledge that a real death occurred. O'Connor does not romanticize death.

While forcing readers to acknowledge hypocrisy, accept reality, face frightening events, and admit God's control, O'Connor does not indulge a reader's cheap curiosity with her immodest material. She exposes hearts and folly instead of covering the deeper issue by titillating a reader's senses. She captivates with reality, not with illusions of pleasure or brainless bliss. Provoking introspection, O'Connor's material is far from sensational as she exhibits

character in her characters.

SAMPLE
ESSAY
EVALUATION
FORM

Lesson Seven

Evaluate the student's essay using the following criteria as a guide; a scoring section follows this chart.

Level 6	Level 5	Level 4	Level 3	Level 2	Level 1
Insightful - Outstanding	Effective - Solid	Competent - Adequate	Inadequate - Limited	Seriously flawed	Deficient
Convincing development of a position on the issue	Proficient, coherent development of a position on the issue	Workmanlike development of a position on the issue	Sketchy development of a position on the issue	Limited development of a position on the issue	Lack of a position on the issue
Selection of relevant examples and evidence to support writer's position	Selection of basically relevant evidence to support writer's position	Selection of reasonably appropriate evidence to support writer's position	Selection of weak or inappropriate evidence to support writer's position	Selection of weak or inappropriate evidence to support writer's position	Absence of evidence to support a point of view
Smooth, well-orchestrated progression from idea to idea	Relatively well-ordered progression from idea to idea	Acceptable progression from idea to idea	Erratic progression from idea to idea	Tendency toward incoherence	Absence of focus and organization
Use of varied sentence types and appropriate vocabulary	Reasonably varied sentence structure and reasonable vocabulary	Somewhat varied sentence structure and somewhat varied vocabulary	Somewhat limited vocabulary and inadequately varied sentence structure	Highly limited vocabulary and numerous problems with sentence structure	Rudimentary vocabulary and severe problems with sentence structure
Freedom from most technical flaws (grammar, usage, diction)	Relative freedom from technical flaws	Some flaws in mechanics, usage, and grammar	Multiple flaws in mechanics, usage, and grammar	Errors in mechanics, usage, and grammar serious enough to interfere with the reader's comprehension	Extensive flaws in mechanics, usage, and grammar severe enough to block the reader's comprehension

(Barron's 301, Kaplan 21, Official 105)

Level 6: demonstrates a clear command of writing and thinking skills despite the occasional, infrequent minor error.

Level 5: exhibits a generally dependable command of writing and thinking skills despite some mistakes.

Level 4: exhibits a generally adequate command of writing and thinking skills although the skills are typically inconsistent in quality.

Level 3: exhibits an insufficient command of writing and thinking skills although the skills show some signs of developing proficiency.

Level 2: exhibits a quite flawed command of writing and thinking skills.

Level 1: exhibits an acutely flawed command of writing and thinking skills.

Student's score of essay (between 1 and 6) _____

[Based on criteria and assignment length, the SAT evaluator's score for this essay is 6].

LESSON EIGHT

PROOFREADING,
PUBLISHING,
AND PRESENTING
THE RESEARCH
PORTFOLIO

A. Concepts

**Lesson Eight
Overview**

1. Proofing

2. Publishing

3. Presenting the Research Portfolio

B. Assignments

1. Collaborative learning interview: evaluator

2. Research language: *proofread, publish, research portfolio*

3. Research Portfolio

4. Evaluations

5. SAT prep prompts: grammar, diction, and usage—
identifying sentence errors; essay writing

6. Sample essay

CONCEPTS

PROOFREADING,
PUBLISHING,
AND
PRESENTING
THE RESEARCH
PORTFOLIO

Honing In

In Lesson Seven you reached significant milestones with the writing of your research: formatting, revising, editing, and peer reviewing. Both you and your peer reviewer took your paper through several checkpoints to bring it closer to perfection. You are ready for the grand finale. All that remains is proofreading and publishing. Caution: Do not stop now! What you do next determines whether your paper soars to phenomenal heights in anticipation of a smooth landing or crashes into a heap of rubble. You are about to use two media to proof your paper: the computer screen and the hardcopy (a printed paper copy). Loeberger defines proofreading, in its strictest sense, as "the inspection and marking of proofs during the printing process. As such, proofreaders are concerned not only with grammatical errors, but also with such issues as spacing, leading, alignment," etc. (284). His statement gives you the background for the term proofreading. In this research paper, you proof-read in a less stringent manner, but in a vital one, nevertheless. Revising and editing should have cleared up most, if not all, structural and grammatical errors. Proofing is your opportunity to make your paper look appealing and professional to your readers. You do not want your thoughts and hard work to be discredited because of what some call a "sloppy copy."

Proofing on the Computer Screen

Take another careful read through your paper as it appears on the screen. Besides all the checkpoints—global and detailed—watch for formatting problems. You may be tempted to pay attention only to those errors highlighted by your computer program. You must be very careful not to rely solely on those even though they give you a good place to begin. Often, computer programs do not follow standard English, are limited in grammatical structures, and advise you to perform a language function that is inaccurate. Keep a comprehensive grammar handbook and dictionary beside you as you edit and proofread. Note the following tips for proofing on screen:

Proofing on the Computer Screen

Global View: Check cover page, outline, headers, pagination, sentences, paragraphs, introduction, conclusion, Works Cited, and any other element for accuracy and position.

Detailed View: Check for punctuation, spacing, spelling, typographical errors, precision and completeness in in-text citations and in Works Cited page.

Hint: Start at the end of your paper and scroll up, reading the paper backwards. You may find more inconsistencies when you read out of sequence.

Almost certainly your eyes will not pick up errors from the screen that you will see on a hardcopy. Determine if you are ready to print a proofreader's hardcopy. This copy may be your third printed copy, or it may be one of several others, but this one is crucial. You are searching for point robbers. Having a pretend-like-it's-for-the-instructor copy now will serve you well.

This copy becomes your final attempt to find lurking anomalies that rob you of your best work. As you read the paper the final time, use the margins to advise yourself on any needed changes. If you are the only one proofing your paper, you can use personal markings that mean something to you but that no one else would understand. However, if you are peer reviewing someone else's paper, learn to use the following fairly standard editorial signs and symbols. Know that there are many other editorial markings used in professional publishing, but the following will suffice for you at this point.

Proofing a Hardcopy

Delete. Something must be removed—single letter, word or words, or entire line without substituting anything else.

Typical Proofreading Symbols

Close up. Too much space between letters or between words.

 Close up and delete. Deleting a letter or letters within a word and then closing the space.

Omission. Draw the caret symbol between letters, words, phrases, or sentences when something has been left out. Write in the omitted information and draw the caret in the margin.

Parallelism. Draw the parallelism symbol in the margin to indicate unparallel words, phrases, or thoughts.

 Superfluous punctuation. Draw a small circle around the superfluous punctuation and draw the symbol in the margin.

 Stet. Let stand; your previous suggestion should be disregarded. To clarify what text should remain unchanged, place dots under the incorrectly marked word or words.

Insert a space. Use to indicate that a space should be added; place a caret in the text where the space should be inserted.

 Transpose. Use to indicate that words or letters or phrases are out of order; write tr in the margin.

 Begin a new paragraph. Place this symbol in the margin to indicate that a paragraph should be broken into two.

 Run-in. Write run-in in the margin and draw a line from the end of the one paragraph to the beginning of the next to indicate that the two paragraphs should be combined.

 Spell out. Circle abbreviations or numerals that should be spelled out and place the symbol in the margin.

ital **Set in italic type.** Draw a single line under the word you want to italicize and write ital in the margin.

bf **Set in boldface type.** Draw a wavy line under the word you want boldfaced and write bf in the margin.

Use the following checkpoints as a guide for your hardcopy proofreading:

**Proofing
a Paper Hardcopy**

Global View: Check cover page, outline, headers, pagination, sentences, paragraphs, introduction, conclusion, Works Cited, and any other element for accuracy and position.

Detailed View: Check for punctuation, spacing, spelling, typographical errors, precision and completeness in in-text citations and in Works Cited page.

Hint: Start at the end of your paper and read backwards. You may find more inconsistencies when you read out of sequence.

Final provision: Read aloud your entire paper from beginning to end. Enjoy the fruits of your labor!

When you are satisfied that your paper is error free, that it supports your thesis, that it represents your attitude (position) toward the subject, that it leaves your readers with a favorable impression of you as a researcher and as a writer, and that it causes your readers to be glad they have read your work, you are ready for the final act of researched writing—publishing your paper for your audience.

Publish

This moment is what you have worked so diligently for during your forty days of researched writing. Everything is checked, double-checked, verified, revised, edited, reviewed, and proofed, and you push the print button to publish your scholarly work for your intended audience for this auspicious occasion. Whether this publication is your first or fifth research paper, you know that you have done quality work, you have done it well, and you have done it with confidence.

Present the Research Portfolio

After publishing your paper for your audience, you are ready to conclude the Research Portfolio. File the remaining evaluation forms and the published copy of your researched writing in their allotted places. When you make the appointment with your evaluator for the final exit interview, present the Research Portfolio as a completed project. Review your published paper, but also review the entire portfolio to see your growth as a writer and as a researcher.

ASSIGNMENTS

PROOFREADING,
PUBLISHING,
AND
PRESENTING
THE RESEARCH
PORTFOLIO

1. Proofreading, publishing, and presenting the research portfolio

A. Read all the information in this lesson.

B. Spend a few hours proofreading and making final corrections in your paper.

C. Read aloud your finished paper.

D. Publish your paper for your audience.

**Collaborative
Learning
Interview**

2. Collaborative learning interview with your evaluator. Enter into a collaborative learning experience by arranging for an exit interview with your research evaluator.

Step A: Arrange to give your evaluator your finished paper several days before you ask for an exit interview—by the end of the eighth week of research. Courteously state your reasons for requesting the interview: you have completed researching a project and are interested in the evaluator's perspectives on your paper and your Research Portfolio.

Step B: Plan what you need to know, especially the specifics the evaluator will have about your paper. Consider using the Evaluation Forms and the Checkpoints.

Step C: Ask about the evaluator's experience with evaluating your research—what your strengths and weaknesses are in researched writing and the portfolio and what you might do differently to improve another project.

Step D: Be respectful, sensitive, and courteous. You are taking valuable time which is being graciously granted to you. Express your appreciation by writing thank-you notes to your teacher, the librarian, the writers and researchers you interviewed, and your peer reviewer for their help with this project.

Step E: Collaborate with your evaluator to organize an audience for the formal presentation of your Research Portfolio.

Evaluations

3. Evaluations: Through evaluation you identify what you already know, what you don't know at all, and what you need to learn. Making these distinctions is part of the metacognitive knowledge dimension—higher-level thinking. Realizing what you don't know is one of the prerequisites for learning.

A. Both you and your teacher should independently complete a final *Research Evaluation Form* and an *Essay Evaluation Form;* yours is located at the end of this lesson.

B. Compare the forms to gain perspective about your experience with this part of the research learning process and with the writing process. Consider reviewing these forms as part of your exit interview.

C. Insert the forms into the Evaluations Section of your Research Portfolio. After you have received the final evaluation of your researched writing, review your Research Portfolio to determine the progress in your writing. Each week you have evaluated yourself with two different evaluation forms: the research process and the written essay. Use those forms with your evaluator during the exit interview to verify your growth as a writer.

4. Research language: Define the following terms using the information in this lesson, in the Appendix, and in a dictionary if necessary: *proofread, publish, research portfolio.* Add these terms, labeled and dated, to the Research Terms section in your Research Portfolio.

Research Language

5. Research Portfolio: Complete organizing and labeling your three-ringed binder with its 5 major divisions—Interviews, Research Language, Evaluations, Essays, and Research Project. (See Appendix G)

Research Portfolio

Review this completed portfolio with your teacher as part of your exit interview and then present it formally to a pre-arranged audience.

RESEARCH EVALUATION FORM: STUDENT

Lesson Eight

Student _____

Date _____

Evaluator _____

Concepts: proofreading, publishing, and presenting the Research Portfolio

	Possible Points	*Earned Points*
Concept readings completed	(20 points)	_____
Proofreading of research writing completed	(20 points)	_____
Read aloud of final paper completed	(10 points)	_____
Exit interview with evaluator completed	(20 points)	_____
Presentation of Research Portfolio after exit interview	(20 points)	_____
Student evaluation completed	(5 points)	_____
Teacher evaluation completed	(5 points)	_____

If you don't fully understand the concepts in this lesson, please review them before you publish the final paper and present the Research Portfolio.

Student's Self-Score for *Lesson Eight* _____

6. SAT Preparation Prompts

The following SAT section will help prepare you for the Scholastic Aptitude Test, a standard college entrance exam. In 2005 the SAT was revised to include additional requirements in the English field. Completing these sections in each lesson will help prepare you for this test and will also enhance your thinking and writing skills. According to *The Official SAT Study Guide for the New SAT* (99), there are three types of multiple-choice questions: identifying sentence errors, improving sentences, and improving paragraphs. Forty-nine questions on grammar and usage test your ability to use language in a consistently clear manner and to improve writing by the use of revision and editing. The multiple-choice questions don't ask you to define or use grammatical terms and don't test spelling or capitalization. Punctuation helps you know the correct answer. Because of these additions to the SAT, this curriculum includes practice with identifying sentence errors and improving sentences.

Grammar, diction, and usage equals two-thirds of your writing score on the SAT. The essay portion equals the other one-third.

Grammar, Diction, and Usage: Identifying Sentence Errors

The sentences in this section may contain errors in grammar, usage, choice of words, or idioms. Either there is just one error in a sentence or the sentence is correct. Some words or phrases are underlined and lettered; everything else in the sentence is correct.

If an underlined word or phrase is incorrect, choose that letter; if the sentence is correct, select <u>No error</u>. Then blacken the appropriate space.

1. <u>For the chivalric gentleman who</u> might be worthy of loving a lady, there could be no
          A
indication of jealousy, <u>the destructive force of love,</u> <u>nor</u> of anything earthly or temporary which
                          B   C
might devalue <u>that love.</u> <u>No error.</u>
              D   E

(A) (B) (C) (D) (E)

2. <u>Even while</u> England was initiating, revising, ignoring, <u>and then reinstating</u> these Arthurian
   A   B
and chivalric <u>concepts, other</u> countries <u>begin</u> to fit the same ideals to their own interests.
                     C   D

(A) (B) (C) (D) (E)

3. The current <u>problem, stated</u> by both the Macklin children and the doctor on the <u>rehab staff, is</u>
                    A   B
Mr. <u>Macklin's unwillingness</u> to consider <u>an alternative discharge plan</u>. <u>No error</u>.
          C   D   E

(A) (B) (C) (D) (E)

4. Structural <u>therapy also breaks</u> families down into subsystems and <u>analyzes</u> the <u>boundaries, that</u>
                    A   B   C
<u>regulate</u> the contact that family <u>members have</u> with each other. <u>No error</u>.
   D   E

(A) (B) (C) (D) (E)

7. SAT Essay Writing

The SAT "assesses your ability to develop and express ideas effectively; [it] evaluate[s] your ability to do the kind of writing required in college—writing that develops a point of view, presents ideas logically and clearly, and uses precise language . . . [the essay is] written in a limited time, which doesn't allow for many revisions, so it is considered and scored as a first draft" (Official 99).

Use this curriculum to prepare for the revised edition of the SAT, which includes writing and grammar elements in addition to three critical reading sections. Use the following pages dedicated to essay writing; they will help you organize and write your thoughts into essay format. Evaluation forms follow: one for you, and one for the sample SAT essay.

Successful writing includes:

1. A clearly expressed thesis statement

2. Well-developed ideas with relevant and accurate supporting information

3. Good organization

4. Appropriate, accurate, and varied vocabulary

5. Variety of sentence structure (syntax)

(Official 106)

The SAT allows you 46 lines on which to write between 300 and 400 words in a persuasive essay. It is important to write legibly because graders will spend approximately one to two minutes reading your essay. They will not spend time trying to decipher your handwriting. Use your two pages wisely, not writing in large letters or leaving extra wide margins. Your goal is to persuade your reader of your position.

**Planning
Essay Eight**

Allot three to five minutes to think about and plan the essay. Make sure you understand the statement and then take a position.

Write about the following statement in two pages; you have *no more than twenty-five minutes.*

Choose between contrasting statements:

> *Publishing newly discovered information gifts society with relevant understanding.
> Publishing newly discovered information burdens society with relevant understanding.*

<u>Assignment</u>: Consider the statements above. Choose the one that best represents your beliefs and write an essay explaining your choice. You may use examples from history, literature, popular culture, current events, or personal experience to support your position.

Which statement do I most agree with?

_____

_____

Reasons/support/evidence for my position (why I agree with it):

I. Example from history, literature, popular culture, current events, or personal experience:

_____

_____

II. Example from history, literature, popular culture, current events, or personal experience:

_____

_____

III. Example from history, literature, popular culture, current events, or personal experience:

_____

_____

_____

These thoughts become the outline for your essay. Do not take more than three to five minutes to organize these thoughts. These first _three to five minutes are crucial to the thinking skills_ you will exhibit in the essay.

You will need the _next twenty minutes to persuade your audience_ of your position on the issue, to support your position as you move from idea to idea, and to use appropriate vocabulary and varied sentence structure free from grammar, mechanics, and usage errors.

It is important not to change your position in the middle of the essay because you won't have time to rework the essay.

You are now ready to write the essay on two sheets of paper. Your goal is to write between 300 and 400 words on the issue.

It is very important to _time the writing_.

Publishing (Gifts or Burdens)
Essay Eight

Your Title:

_____

_____

_____

_____

_____

_____

_____

_____

_____

_____

_____

_____

_____

_____

_____

_____

_____

_____

_____

_____

_____

Evaluate your essay using the following criteria as a guide; a scoring section follows this chart.

Lesson Eight

PRACTICE ESSAY
EVALUATION
FORM:
STUDENT

211

Lesson Eight

Level 6	Level 5	Level 4	Level 3	Level 2	Level 1
Insightful - Outstanding	Effective - Solid	Competent - Adequate	Inadequate - Limited	Seriously flawed	Deficient
Convincing development of a position on the issue	Proficient, coherent development of a position on the issue	Workmanlike development of a position on the issue	Sketchy development of a position on the issue	Limited development of a position on the issue	Lack of a position on the issue
Selection of relevant examples and evidence to support writer's position	Selection of basically relevant evidence to support writer's position	Selection of reasonably appropriate evidence to support writer's position	Selection of weak or inappropriate evidence to support writer's position	Selection of weak or inappropriate evidence to support writer's position	Absence of evidence to support a point of view
Smooth, well-orchestrated progression from idea to idea	Relatively well-ordered progression from idea to idea	Acceptable progression from idea to idea	Erratic progression from idea to idea	Tendency toward incoherence	Absence of focus and organization
Use of varied sentence types and appropriate vocabulary	Reasonably varied sentence structure and reasonable vocabulary	Somewhat varied sentence structure and somewhat varied vocabulary	Somewhat limited vocabulary and inadequately varied sentence structure	Highly limited vocabulary and numerous problems with sentence structure	Rudimentary vocabulary and severe problems with sentence structure
Freedom from most technical flaws (grammar, usage, diction)	Relative freedom from technical flaws	Some flaws in mechanics, usage, and grammar	Multiple flaws in mechanics, usage, and grammar	Errors in mechanics, usage, and grammar serious enough to interfere with the reader's comprehension	Extensive flaws in mechanics, usage, and grammar severe enough to block the reader's comprehension

(Barron's 301, Kaplan 21, Official 105)

Level 6: demonstrates a clear command of writing and thinking skills despite the occasional, infrequent minor error.
Level 5: exhibits a generally dependable command of writing and thinking skills despite some mistakes.
Level 4: exhibits a generally adequate command of writing and thinking skills although the skills are typically inconsistent in quality.
Level 3: exhibits an insufficient command of writing and thinking skills although the skills show some signs of developing proficiency.
Level 2: exhibits a quite flawed command of writing and thinking skills.
Level 1: exhibits an acutely flawed command of writing and thinking skills.

Student's self-score of essay (between 1 and 6) _____

**Sample
Student
Essay**

Read the following essay and then determine the score you would give it based on the scoring criteria and word count. Using literary analysis, this student responds (in less than 500 words) to the following SAT Essay prompt. Evidently the student could write profusely on this topic because of previous studies that could be adapted to fit the prompt.

Respond to the following statement:

> *International, national, or personal affairs often hinge on relationships and personalities.*
> *This phenomenon is illustrated in* _____.

<u>Assignment</u>: The statement above implies that interpersonal skills have the power to influence events beyond the present. Do you agree or disagree? Write a persuasive essay supporting, disputing, or qualifying the statement. You may use examples from history, literature, popular culture, current events, or personal experience to support your position.

Relationship in Dickens' *A Tale of Two Cities*

The relationship in *A Tale of Two Cities* between the Evremonde brothers and Doctor Mannette discloses some of the deepest inner-workings of the human heart. The Evremondes take an attractive peasant girl from her family, after killing her husband, and they rape her. When her brother seeks revenge, he is also murdered. When the brothers realize that their molested victim is dying because of her physical and emotional trauma, they kidnap the Doctor to care for her. He learns the terrible story of the peasant girl's tragedy, and after the girl finally perishes, he writes a letter to the Minister explaining the crimes. Of course the brothers intercept the documentation of their deeds and promptly imprison Dr. Mannette. These two encounters between the Evremondes and the Doctor subtly expose the connection between their hearts and their actions.

All three of these characters lived in their own created unrealities. The brothers imagined away any pity and sensitivity toward their fellow human beings dressed as peasants. They refused to consider that those born into a lower class were anything but just that: lower, worthy only of being trampled under foot. Being so deluded with their own power, the Evremonde brothers could even ignore the consequences for committing such a brutal violation against the peasant girl and her family. All morality was abandoned in the created world of their minds.

Dr. Mannette lived in quite a different unreality than the brothers. In his world, a simple letter explaining horrific injustices was to be received by men who, like the Doctor, wanted to do what was right. His confidence in justice being served led Dr. Mannette to make an upstanding choice by reporting severe crimes; however, this justice fantasy severely backfired on him, and in retaliation he again made a grave mistake through his imagination: he narrated the fatal night he was captured to look after the raped girl. Rather than simply retelling the unjust reasons for his sentence, he zealously denounced the entire Evremonde family and all of its descendants. The Doctor's severe depression forbade his mind to explore his harshness and insensitivity to upcoming generations having nothing to do with the violations. Despite just anger, Dr. Mannette proclaimed damnation on the Evremonde lineage.

The actual relationship between the brothers and the Doctor is tense and only in passing: in passing from Dr. Mannette's home to see the dying girl and then back again, and later in passing from his home to the Bastille prison, for an eighteen year sentence. They speak little to each other and understand each other even less. However, for the few days they know each other, the three men make enormous moral decisions regarding one another. They acted out of their perceptions of the world around them. How sad, then, that they perceived the world falsely and either acted immorally, or in the case of Dr. Mannette's reporting the crimes, morally but ignorantly to bring such great ramifications even to unborn generations.

Evaluate the student's essay using the following criteria as a guide; a scoring section follows this chart.

SAMPLE ESSAY EVALUATION FORM

Lesson Eight

Level 6	Level 5	Level 4	Level 3	Level 2	Level 1
Insightful - Outstanding	Effective - Solid	Competent - Adequate	Inadequate - Limited	Seriously flawed	Deficient
Convincing development of a position on the issue	Proficient, coherent development of a position on the issue	Workmanlike development of a position on the issue	Sketchy development of a position on the issue	Limited development of a position on the issue	Lack of a position on the issue
Selection of relevant examples and evidence to support the writer's position	Selection of basically relevant evidence to support the writer's position	Selection of reasonably appropriate evidence to support the writer's position	Selection of weak or inappropriate evidence to support the writer's position	Selection of weak or inappropriate evidence to support the writer's position	Absence of evidence to support a point of view
Smooth, well-orchestrated progression from idea to idea	Relatively well-ordered progression from idea to idea	Acceptable progression from idea to idea	Erratic progression from idea to idea	Tendency toward incoherence	Absence of focus and organization
Use of varied sentence types and appropriate vocabulary	Reasonably varied sentence structure and reasonable vocabulary	Somewhat varied sentence structure and somewhat varied vocabulary	Somewhat limited vocabulary and inadequately varied sentence structure	Highly limited vocabulary and numerous problems with sentence structure	Rudimentary vocabulary and severe problems with sentence structure
Freedom from most technical flaws (grammar, usage, diction)	Relative freedom from technical flaws	Some flaws in mechanics, usage, and grammar	Multiple flaws in mechanics, usage, and grammar	Errors in mechanics, usage, and grammar serious enough to interfere with the reader's comprehension	Extensive flaws in mechanics, usage, and grammar severe enough to block the reader's comprehension

(Barron's 301, Kaplan 21, Official 105)

Level 6: demonstrates a clear command of writing and thinking skills despite the occasional, infrequent minor error.
Level 5: exhibits a generally dependable command of writing and thinking skills despite some mistakes.
Level 4: exhibits a generally adequate command of writing and thinking skills although the skills are typically inconsistent in quality.
Level 3: exhibits an insufficient command of writing and thinking skills although the skills show some signs of developing proficiency.
Level 2: exhibits a quite flawed command of writing and thinking skills.
Level 1: exhibits an acutely flawed command of writing and thinking skills.

Student's score of sample essay (between 1 and 6) _____
[Based on criteria and assignment length, the SAT evaluator's score for this essay is 6].

Congratulations!

	DATE	COMPLETED
WEEK ONE:		
Monday:	_____	_____
Tuesday:	_____	_____
Wednesday:	_____	_____
Thursday:	_____	_____
Friday:	_____	_____
WEEK TWO:		
Monday:	_____	_____
Tuesday:	_____	_____
Wednesday:	_____	_____
Thursday:	_____	_____
Friday:	_____	_____
WEEK THREE:		
Monday:	_____	_____
Tuesday:	_____	_____
Wednesday:	_____	_____
Thursday:	_____	_____
Friday:	_____	_____
WEEK FOUR:		
Monday:	_____	_____
Tuesday:	_____	_____
Wednesday:	_____	_____
Thursday:	_____	_____
Friday:	_____	_____

APPENDIX "A"

Timeline for Research—Eight Weeks

For students relatively new to research and who have an average academic load

Notes and Reminders:

**Notes and
Reminders:**

	DATE	COMPLETED
WEEK FIVE:		
Monday:	_____	_____
Tuesday:	_____	_____
Wednesday:	_____	_____
Thursday:	_____	_____
Friday:	_____	_____
WEEK SIX:		
Monday:	_____	_____
Tuesday:	_____	_____
Wednesday:	_____	_____
Thursday:	_____	_____
Friday:	_____	_____
WEEK SEVEN:		
Monday:	_____	_____
Tuesday:	_____	_____
Wednesday:	_____	_____
Thursday:	_____	_____
Friday:	_____	_____
WEEK EIGHT:		
Monday:	_____	_____
Tuesday:	_____	_____
Wednesday:	_____	_____
Thursday:	_____	_____
Friday:	_____	_____

	DATE	COMPLETED
WEEK ONE:		
Monday:	_____	_____
Tuesday:	_____	_____
Wednesday:	_____	_____
Thursday:	_____	_____
Friday:	_____	_____
WEEK TWO:		
Monday:	_____	_____
Tuesday:	_____	_____
Wednesday:	_____	_____
Thursday:	_____	_____
Friday:	_____	_____
WEEK THREE:		
Monday:	_____	_____
Tuesday:	_____	_____
Wednesday:	_____	_____
Thursday:	_____	_____
Friday:	_____	_____
WEEK FOUR:		
Monday:	_____	_____
Tuesday:	_____	_____
Wednesday:	_____	_____
Thursday:	_____	_____
Friday:	_____	_____

APPENDIX "B"

Timeline for Research—Four Weeks

For students who have experience with research or who have a relatively light academic load

Notes and Reminders:

APPENDIX "C"

Example of Working Outline

I. Week One: Introduction to researched writing

Concepts: Need for research; higher-level thinking skills; form of communication; research overview; choosing a subject and investigating

Activities: Collaborative learning interviews; writing logs; SAT preparation prompts; evaluations

II. Week Two: Preliminaries

Concepts: Timelines and deadlines; library familiarization; availability of information; writing log; gathering and recording information; contemplating the subject and research question; library exploration; computer research; validity and reliability; audience

Activities: Interviews and essays; SAT; writing logs; evaluations; portfolio

III. Week Three: Processes

Concepts: Reading, jotting, investigating, reflecting, organizing; limiting the subject; audience; thesis; outlining; audience

Activities: Interviews and essays; SAT; writing logs; evaluations; portfolio

IV. Week Four: Drafting and revising

Concepts: Outlining; reading; investigating; reflecting; reorganizing; introducing; transitioning; audience

Activities: Interviews and essays; SAT; writing logs; evaluations; portfolio

V. Week Five: Drafting and revising

Concepts: Paragraphing; concluding; revising; audience

Activities: Interviews and essays; SAT; writing logs; evaluations; portfolio

VI. Week Six: Drafting and revising

    Concepts: Structural elements; effectiveness; mechanics; punctuation; spelling; diction

    Activities: Interviews and essays; SAT; writing logs; evaluations; portfolio

VII. Week Seven: Drafting and revising

    Concepts: Formatting and revising

    Activities: Interviews and essays; SAT; writing logs; evaluations; portfolio

VIII. Week Eight: Printing, revising, publishing

    Concepts: Formatting; revising; publishing; proofreading; revising; publishing

    Activities: Interviews and essays; SAT; writing logs; evaluations; portfolio

APPENDIX "D"

Example of Final Outline

I. Lesson One: introducing *Writing Research*

  A. Concepts

    1. Lesson overview

    2. Background

    3. Reasons for research

    4. Library familiarity

    5. Writing and thinking

    6. Higher-level thinking skills

      a. Knowledge dimensions

      b. Cognitive process dimensions

  B. Assignments

    1. Preparation for research

    2. Research portfolio

    3. Research language: *knowledge dimensions, cognitive process dimensions, on-line, card catalog, Dewey Decimal System, Library of Congress System, computerized catalog, electronic databases, CD-ROM, research, communication, style, essay, library, reference, source, write*

    4. Collaborative learning interview: professional librarian

    5. Evaluations

    6. SAT preparation prompts: grammar, diction, and usage— identifying sentence errors; essay writing

    7. Sample essays

II. Lesson Two: initiating writing research

  A. Concepts

    1. Timeline and deadlines

    2. Library and computer familiarity

    3. Developing a working bibliography

APPENDIX "D"

Example of Final Outline

4. Choosing the subject or research question

5. Formulating a thesis statement

6. Audience

B. Assignments

1. Collaborative learning interview: friend or family researcher

2. Research language: *thesis, audience, bibliography, working bibliography, hypothesis, enthymeme, periodical, Works Cited, style manuals*

3. Research portfolio

4. Evaluations

5. SAT prep prompts: grammar, diction, and usage—identifying sentence errors; essay writing

6. Sample essay

ETC. . . . (found at the beginning of this book as Scope and Sequence)

APPENDIX "E"

Sample Note Card

Williams, ed. <u>Annals Cambriae</u>
pp. 85-87

I. A.

Written on this 4x6 card will be a summary of information from pages 85-87 of the book *Annals Cambriae*, written by Williams. If the information were a direct quotation, instead of a summary or paraphrase, it would contain quotation marks around the information so that later, after I've taken many other notes, I will remember that this one is a direct quotation. Note the **I. A.** in the upper right-hand corner. That code tells me that this note coordinates with point A under Major Heading I in my outline. If I drop my note cards and they get disordered, I will have a system for organizing them again. I continue with this process of note identification throughout my entire research project. Taking only one note on each card keeps the information clearly related to its topic and prevents my losing notes that are mixed in with other information.

Sample Bibliography Card

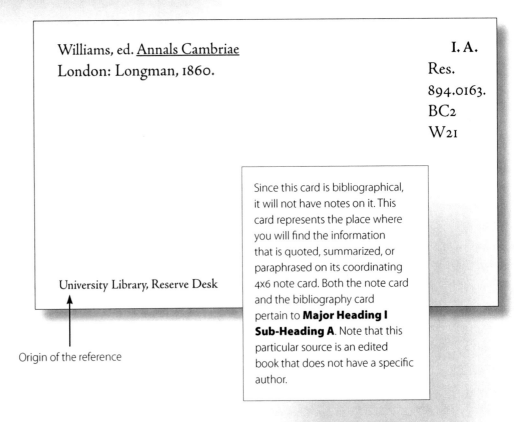

Williams, ed. <u>Annals Cambriae</u>
London: Longman, 1860.

I. A.
Res.
894.0163.
BC2
W21

University Library, Reserve Desk

Origin of the reference

Since this card is bibliographical, it will not have notes on it. This card represents the place where you will find the information that is quoted, summarized, or paraphrased on its coordinating 4x6 note card. Both the note card and the bibliography card pertain to **Major Heading I Sub-Heading A**. Note that this particular source is an edited book that does not have a specific author.

APPENDIX
"F"

**Research
Portfolio Cover
Page**

*Needed if you are
asked to submit your
final outline with your
research paper*

Title of Research

Student
Date

Educator
Course Name
Umbrella School
Address
Contact Information

APPENDIX
"G"

**Research
Portfolio
Contents**

Contents

SECTION ONE: Interviews—labeled and dated

SECTION TWO: Research Language—labeled and dated

SECTION THREE: Evaluations—labeled and dated

SECTION FOUR: SAT Practice Essays—labeled and dated

SECTION FIVE: Research Project

1. Cover Page

2. Final Detailed Outline

3. Paper

4. Works Cited

5. Note cards in front pocket

6. Bibliography cards in back pocket

**Partial List
of Manuals
for Research,
Writing,
Grammar, and
SAT Preparation**

Chicago Manual of Style. The Fifteenth Edition. Chicago: U of Chicago P, 2003.

Gibaldi, Joseph. MLA Handbook for Writers of Research Papers, Sixth Edition. New York: MLA of America, 2004.

Green, Sharon Weiner, and Ira K Wolf. How to Prepare for the New SAT. 22nd ed. New York: Barron's Educational Series, 2005.

Hodges, John C., Winifred Bryan Horner, Suzanne Strobeck Webb, and Robert Keith Miller. Harbrace College Handbook, Revised Thirteenth Edition with 1998 MLA Manual Updates. New York: Harcourt, 1998.

Kaplan Test Preparation and Admissions. The New SAT Critical Reading Workbook. New York: Simon & Schuster, 2004.

Lester, James D., Sr., and James D. Lester, Jr. Writing Research Papers: A Complete Guide. New York: Longman, 2005.

Loberger, Gordon, and Kate Shoup Welsh. Webster's New World English Grammar Handbook. IN: Wiley Pub, 2002.

Official SAT Study Guide for the New SAT. New York: College Board, 2004.

Sabin, William A. The Gregg Reference Manual, Ninth Edition. Peoria: Glencoe McGraw-Hill, 2001.

Sebranek, Patrick, Verne Meyer, and Dave Kemper. Writer's Inc. Write for College: A Student Handbook. Wilmington: Great Source Education Group, Houghton, 1997.

APPENDIX "I"

Student Research Paper with Heading and Works Cited

Sample #1

Student paper is to be 8½" x 11" with all type 12 point double-spaced and 1" margins all around.

Sophomore Student **[Double spaces between all lines throughout.]**

British Literature

Dr. Ruth Maestra

April 12, 2005

Something Long Lost: Dickens' Portrayal of Childhood Pain in *A Tale of Two Cities*

In *A Tale of Two Cities* Charles Dickens explores both children's experiences of and their reactions to pain and suffering. **[Introductory sentence sets the scene for the paper]** While the key characters in this story are all adults, Dickens provides brief flashbacks into their earlier years and exposes the foundations on which these characters are built. The few paragraphs allotted to the young Charles Darnay and to the child Madame Therese Defarge furnish insights into their needs as children. The nourishment, or lack of nourishment, of these needs creates the conditions in which the children live and to which they respond. Dickens records his own life experiences through chronicling his characters' needs, the negligence or nourishment of these needs, and the characters' reactions to how these needs are considered. **[Thesis statement]**

Donovan's observation that "Many of Dickens' fictional children who were not mistreated were often misunderstood" describes Charles Darnay exactly (17). **[Direct quotation from source by Donovan, page 17, worked into the text and providing source information].** In the midst of **[transitional phrase]** opposing parental influences, the young Darnay lacks the nurturing support of a loving family. His criminal father offers a despicable example of paternal protection and reassurance, and he exposes the boy prematurely to the world's evil. Darnay carries deep shame over the horrible crimes against the peasant people. He is bombarded with extreme expectations to grow into the family name and to carry on the Evremonde pride by oppressing the lower class. Donovan captures this family cycle by stating that "What the younger [boy] was then, the elder had been once; and what the elder then was, the younger must soon become" (9). **[Direct quotation from source by Donovan, page 9, worked into the text; [boy] is clarification information added by the writer of the paper and is not in the original material].** It was assumed by his family and social class that Charles would grow to be exactly like his father, despite whatever personality differences they may have. His needs to search for his own identity are not even considered. Fortunately **[transition]**, Darnay's compassionate mother provides the maternal love and acceptance he uses to resist following his father's footsteps. Acting in her son's best interest, **[transitional phrase]** she gives everything she has to keep Charles safe and to provide for his future. Yet while his mother nurtures his needs for security and acceptance, Darnay's father looms as a cold, domineering man apt to reject the boy's tender self. The Marquis St. Evremonde demands a son saturated with greed, lust, and power.

In nearly every aspect, Therese Defarge's childhood vastly differs from Darnay's upbringing. Her father prays for barren women since "it [is] a dreadful thing to bring a child into the world" (Dickens 303; bk. 3; ch. 10). **[Direct quotation from Dicken's *A Tale of Two Cities* in book 3, chapter 10, page 303; [is] is added by the writer**

for clarification and is not in the original material]. Though it is in regard to the pain children suffer from a life of poverty that he advocates sterility, his statements no doubt resound confusion and rejection in his youngest daughter. Therese is a small child herself as she hears her father declaring the wretchedness of young life. In her undeveloped mind she would naturally conclude that she is the "dreadful thing" **[Writer uses quotation marks for emphasis and reference to the previously used direct quotation.]** not deserving to live. This unintended rejection of the youth merely compounds the pain. Constantly humiliated by the upper class, Therese learns to survive with little physical nourishment and protection. Her family cannot provide security—they have none to offer. How can they reassure her that she is wanted and loved when the shrunken stomachs scream with the voice of a cruel society that peasants are worthless mongrels? Even if her family could tend to her fragile insecurities, they are brutally murdered early in her life. Enduring this crisis, **[transitional phrase]** Therese must live in hiding with a fisherman's family. The shameful knowledge of her sister's rape is imprinted indelibly on the child's heart. Battered by her unstable early years, she hardly has a chance to overcome her circumstances.

Young Darnay and Therese's early experiences of emotional trauma parallel to their creator's background. How could Dickens have such intimate insight into a child's pain except through personal experience? Chesterton chronicles Dickens' boyhood and youth by describing the author's negligent family. Similar to the Marquis' disregarding of young Darnay, the aloof Mr. John Dickens ignores his own son; his careless approach to finally allowing Charles an education further distances the child from his family. Financial hardships due to his father's shameful imprisonment force the twelve-year-old Dickens to work in a blacking factory. After Charles' release from the harsh, embarrassing factory work, his mother rejects him at home and seeks to keep him employed in the industry (Chesterton 30-55). **[Last name of author Chesterton is repeated in this reference, even though it was mentioned in the text, because it was mentioned several sentences above.]** Mrs. Elizabeth Dickens remains emotionally absent just as Therese Defarge's mother is absent in her daughter's painful years. In his journal Dickens later wrote: "but I never afterwards forgot, I never shall forget, I never can forget, that my mother was warm for my being sent back" (Allen 102). **[Reference includes author's last name and the page since the author's name is not mentioned within the text of the paper.]**

While describing painful childhood in Dickens' novels, **[Transitional phrase ties previous paragraph to this one.]** Donovan notes that "When Dickens describes such a childhood it is usually in terms of *something long lost, or something that might have been*" (15). Dickens goes on to describe the child's search to find what was long lost. Charles Darnay recoiled from his father's example and denounced his wealthy inheritance before seeking what "might have been" by traveling far away from his family. He flees from his childhood physically and emotionally by escaping to England and suppressing the memories of what he leaves behind in France. To replace haughty prestige, Darnay fills his life with honest work and his own dear family. A wife and children fulfill the security and love he lost as a child. Also, the adult Darnay exaggerates generosity and kindness in response to the shame and guilt he carries. Gwen Watkins observes that "At first the question is whether the unwanted can prove their right to exist by being *good*" (124). Darnay seems to follow this thought exactly; with his 'good' over-compensations, however, his positive intentions turn and reject his early feelings of frailty and helplessness. He does not comfort and understand his pain but merely attempts to repay the previously witnessed evil. His rejected soul needs the atonement, but instead it receives an unsatisfying reproach.

This severance **[Transitional phrase ties previous paragraph to this one.]** from his early-self brews unrest underneath Charles' adulthood happiness. Because he cannot reject his young, fragile side forever, Darnay eventually seeks restoration by returning to his homeland. The nightmares of the child Darnay at once spring to life, and he is held accountable by the peasantry for the crimes his father committed. His meager pleas to rectify the past by being generous and kind fall useless to the ground; the helpless child Darnay is once again exposed, shamed, and guilty for simply being his father's son. For so long, Darnay had struggled to deny and distance himself from his upbringing, but these defenses crumble when he revisits his past. Andrews notes, "Children in whom childhood has not naturally ripened, but in whom maturity is forced, are deprived of what Dickens regards as the proper culture of childhood . . . such deprivation produces deformed adults" (4). **[Ellipsis in this sentence indicates that the writer has left out some of the material in the original text that would not be pertinent to this point in the paper.]** The deprived and emotionally deformed Therese grows into the antithesis of Dickens' ideal woman. As the author observes in another story, "What could one poor child do" in the face of such direly shocking circumstances? (Donovan 18). Society rejects her, her family is dead, and she has no one but herself to lean upon. A child cannot handle such burdens and remain precious and innocent. In order to survive, Therese in a sense kills her soul. To feel the pain of losing her family would be to allow her physical heart to burst, leaving her body to die as her father's did. Therefore, she compromises and subconsciously permits her circumstances to crucify only her sensitive, emotional self. Ridding her heart of all sensitivity, she participates in her own soul's murder: "The tiny self," says Karen Horney, "unwittingly takes part" (qtd. in Watkins 107). **[A divided direct quotation from K Horney that is quoted in a secondary source by Watkins, page 107; quoting from primary sources is preferable.]** With the feeling soul deadened, she covers the traces of the crime with overwhelming anger. This anger leads her in the transition from young Therese to hardened adult Madame. Her split selves "are not aware of each other, cannot communicate and therefore can never help or affect each other" (133). **[No author name is provided here because the quote is taken from the previously provided source by Watkins.]** Madame suppresses her second self so severely that it never reappears; while hushing her frailty with the promise for revenge, her sole bitter emotion eventually destroys her (71, 129). **[Summarized reference to two separate pages from the same Watkins source.]**

Through both Darnay and Mme Defarge, Dickens narrates parts of his own reactions to pain. Like Charles Darnay, Dickens stifles the frail remembrances of neglect and rejection. As a child he nurses intense resentment toward his parents for financial and emotional neglect, and he feels that his lack of education is a rejection of his abilities. Similar to **[transitional phrase]** Mme's refusal to ever release her anger, he protects himself by a steadfast determination to share his resentment with no one and to successfully overcome his poverty. Allen observes that Dickens achieves these goals: only eventually does he share his resentment with his wife and his biographer (86-87). **[paraphrased or summarized reference from two pages of material]** He reaches some sense of material success, but at what risk? Watkins states, "In his inner self **[Dickens]** remained always a child deprived of natural growth by the lack of early parental love" and later, "The child who builds himself a second self to gain love and approval needs immense will-power to do so and to keep the true self from breaking through" (9, 84). Dickens builds this second self to be the strong child determined to quiet his pain, to store his resentment, and to be successful in spite of it all. However, later in Dickens' life, his true self insistently breaks through the strict barriers, and he states in a letter that something "is always driving me, and I cannot help it" (18).

While Mme Defarge's stifled self stalks revenge and Darnay's seeks family security, Dickens' repressed soul keeps a constant vigil searching for a suitable maternal figure. As a boy, Dickens spends most of his time separated from his family, and he is not close to his mother. When she attempts to send him back to the factory, the inexpressible rejection he feels completely cuts any ties that bind them. Watkins sheds light on Dickens' relationship with his mother and subsequently with other women:

the mother will also, by what *she* is, give the child an unconscious expectation of what women will be in his adult life: if he sees women as cruel or rejecting, he will either be attracted to women who are so in reality, or will so manouevre (sic) by his own behaviour (sic) women who are not like this, that they will either genuinely reject him or seem to him to do so. (23) **[The writer inserts the term (sic) to indicate that the spelling in the quotation is exact, not an error.]**

Again, **[transitional word]** the themes of searching for "something long lost or something that might have been" shows up in the author's works and personal life, as noted by Benson ("Charles Dickens"). **[Parenthetical Internet notation with author reference.]** Dickens rejects his wife and falls in love with numerous women, including his sister-in-law, who soon dies. He never enters a satisfactory, fulfilling relationship with a woman because the void in his child-heart demands the mother he does not have. Dickens never faces this wound but allows it to dictate the failures of his marriage and courtships ("Charles Dickens").

In exploring so much of the pain endured in childhood and the avenues chosen for dealing with that pain, Dickens reveals distinct survival patterns within Darnay, Mme Defarge, and himself. Both author and characters attempt to stifle the emotions arising from hurtful childhood experiences. Darnay places physical distance between himself and the painful reminders, but Madame Defarge's sole anesthetic for pain is her bitterness. Like her creator, **[transitional phrase]** the woman quietly amasses anger until the lust for revenge infests her. This preservation of hostility buries all sentiment of compassion and gentleness, leaving her an un-sexed victim of brutality. Though Dickens' burial process of his tender emotions never reaches the intensity of Mme's detachment, he sufficiently severs himself from his neglected child-self. This splitting of the selves creates the need for the real-life death of one of these selves ("Charles Dickens"). The rejected child-self cannot coexist with the adult-self neglectful of his own pain. One must die, and it is usually the frail, trembling victim that yields to the commands of the impatient survivor (Watkins 107). **[Since the source's author is not mentioned in the text of the paper, the name is supplied in the parenthetical notation.]** Thus, **[Writer uses repetition for emphasis through transitions in the next three sentences.]** Mme's compassion for humanity dies as her compassion for herself ceases. Thus, Darnay attempts to murder his memories; they resurrect when he returns to France, though, and demand a death in return for his abandoning them. Thus, Dickens fervently works his whole life, becoming a successful, driven, and tormented man: "I have now no relief but in action. I am become incapable of rest. I am quite confident that I should rust, break and die, if I spared myself.... Restlessness, you will say. Whatever it is, it is always driving me, and I cannot help it" (qtd. in Watkins 17-18). **[Writer again uses a secondary source for a quote originally written by Dickens. Good research expects quotations from primary sources unless absolutely impossible. This writer's paper would be more impressive with primary source quotations.]**

Emotional repression, self-severance, and restlessness: these three reactions are consistently present in Dickens' descriptions of childhood hardship. **[Summary listing serves as a reminder to readers of the papers' primary purposes.]** The fictitious experiences of Charles Darnay and Mme Defarge reach much farther than the printed page, though. **[Transitional word "though" ties thoughts and sentences together.]** Dickens uses these experiences to illustrate his own struggles and feelings from his younger years. Since his grappling with early pain is not resolved before adulthood, it repeatedly resurfaces in his novel *A Tale of Two Cities*. **[Writer aptly summarizes in this conclusion paragraph without repeating the introductory paragraph.]**

Works Cited

Allen, Michael. Charles Dickens' Childhood. New York: St. Martin's, 1988.

Andrews, Malcolm. Dickens and the Grown-up Child. London: Macmillan, 1994.

Benson, Kenneth. "Charles Dickens: The Life of the Author." (1997). 12 Feb. 2005

    http://www.fathom.com/course/21701768/session1.html.

Chesterton, G. K. Charles Dickens: A Critical Study. New York: Dodd, 1929.

Dickens, Charles. A Tale of Two Cities. 1850. Foreword Stephen Koch. New York: Bantam, 1981.

Donovan, Frank. Dickens and Youth. New York: Dodd, 1968.

Watkins, Gwen. Dickens in Search of Himself: Recurrent Themes and Characters in the Work of

    Charles Dickens. Totowa: Barnes, 1987.

Some Subjects Addressed in Edna St. Vincent Millay's Sonnets

Student

April 9, 2005

Ms. Deanne Song

American Literature

1234 Education Drive

Special Place, TN 37000

Constance Escuela, Administrator

615-000-1111

11"

8½"

APPENDIX "I"

Student Research Paper with Cover Page, Outline, Text, and Works Cited

Sample #2

Student paper is to be 8½" x 11" with all type 12 point double-spaced and 1" margins all around.

Outline

I. Description of Millay's sonnets

    A. Influences on her sonnet writing

        1. The Renaissance and Romantic periods

        2. Shakespeare

        3. Donne

    B. Topics addressed by her sonnets

        1. Politics

        2. Time

        3. Love

II. The role of gender in the traditional sonnet

    A. Male-dominance

    B. Female suppression

III. Millay's approach to the sonnet

    A. Reasons she wrote sonnets

    B. Ways she challenged the traditional sonnet's male-dominance

IV. Criticism for Millay's sonnets

    A. Negative

        1. Before her death

        2. After her death

    B. Positive

        1. Before her death

        2. After her death

Some Subjects Addressed in Edna St. Vincent Millay's Sonnets
[Double spaces between all lines throughout.]

Many critics agree that Edna St. Vincent Millay's sonnets are her best literary works. She writes in the traditional Petrarchan or Shakespearean forms, with either an octet/sestet or a triple-quatrain/couplet pattern ("Sonnet" 13). **[Article title without an author.]** Millay's various literary influences obviously affect her choice to pursue sonnet writing, though she approaches the sonnet with uncustomary female perspectives. She incorporates her viewpoints into sonnets centered around politics, time, and love. Specifically, in "I Will Put Chaos Into Fourteen Lines" and in sonnet sequences *Fatal Interview* and *Sonnets from an Ungrafted Tree*, Millay boldly challenges the male-dominance hidden in the traditional sonnet form. **[Thesis statement]**

By the time she began her writing career, Millay had become well acquainted with the sonnets of various authors. Her literary influences ranged from the English Renaissance and Romantic writers as a whole to Wordsworth, Donne, and Shakespeare in particular. In the preface to the revised and expanded *Collected Sonnets of Edna St. Vincent Millay*, editor Elizabeth Barnett quotes Millay describing an important guide: "I had read much of the poetry of Wordsworth, and learned by heart several of his shorter poems" (xiii). **[Page numbers found in the preface]** Patricia Klemans notes that in Millay's sonnet sequence *Fatal Interview* there is a heavy reliance on the imagery and philosophy of John Donne's love poetry. In fact, the sequence's title is taken from Donne's "Elegy 16" (Thesing 201). Hubbard recognizes three Millay sonnets that directly allude or respond to Shakespeare's sonnet 73; obviously this great English author had a heavy influence on her writing (Freedman 112). Similarly, Wiltenburg highlights several aspects in which Millay's thinking resembles Renaissance thinking: a "divided sense of humanity's potential exaltation and degradation"; the "fullest sense of a poem's rhythm, tone, and emphasis" that is only available in "speaking and hearing . . . the words on the page"; and the "technical hints and tricks" in poetry dealing with "love, loss, change, loneliness, [and] death" (Thesing 287-89). From these various English movements and authors, Millay drew her much of her philosophy and appreciation for the sonnet.

Edna Millay also imitated [**transition**] these well-known sonneteers by addressing such subjects as politics, time, and love. In "The Woman as Political Poet: Edna St. Vincent Millay and the Mid-Century Canon," John Timberman Newcomb lists Millay's political sonnets. Her "Two Sonnets in Memory" address the Sacco-Vanzetti experience: a legal Massachusetts hanging of two men on whose behalf Millay personally appealed to the governor. Millay also confronts politics and humanity in the sonnet sequence *Epitaph for the Race of Man* (Newcomb 268-69). Regarding the subject of time, critic Robert Johnson provides an extensive discussion of Millay's treatment of time in her sonnets. Johnson describes a Renaissance definition and a Modernist definition of time, citing examples in Millay's sonnets of a combination of the two. He claims that Millay employs the Renaissance time model with subjects and characteristics that "root her *directly* in her age," the age of Modernism (Freedman 127).

While consideration of politics and time is apparent in Millay's sonnets, **[transitional phrase connecting ideas from the outline]** her overriding subject matter is love. From her first book, *Renascence*, to the posthumous *Mine the Harvest*, Millay includes love sonnets in most of her poetry collections (Barnett v-xi). Some of the sonnets describe specific love affairs, as in "I Only Know That Every Hour With You," which refers to her romance with poet Arthur Davison Ficke (Brittin 11). Others, such as the sonnets in the series *Sonnets from an Ungrafted Tree*, relate a fictitious situation involving the death of love in a marriage (52). Millay's longest love sequence, *Fatal Interview*, contains fifty-two sonnets chronicling action spread out over fifty-two weeks, or a whole year. Within the cyclical structure, Millay "demonstrate[s] the emotional life of a woman speaker as she lives out the captured year, each sonnet representing some one moment of insight into a growing, then faltering, apparently extramarital, love affair" (Freedman 124). By Elizabeth Atkins' standards, *Fatal Interview* is "undated poetry" in its treatment of the subjective emotions of a lover--any lover from ancient to modern times (Atkins 199). The fifty-two sonnets are perhaps Millay's culmination of love poetry. **[Sources are freely used to back up the author's position.]**

Millay's ideas for treating the themes of politics, time and love came from her noted literary predecessors, Wordsworth, Shakespeare, and Donne. **[The paper unfolds to parallel the outline.]** They had set the standard for treating these themes in the sonnet; however, in their standard, the poetic forebears subtly wove their own personal and societal discriminations into the sonnet genre. Debra Fried describes these discriminations in her article "Andromeda Unbound: Gender and Genre in Millay's Sonnets" (Thesing 229). She presents the genre as being male-dominant. Through exposition of Wordsworth's "Nuns Fret Not at Their Convent's Narrow Room," Fried describes the role sonnets have customarily played for established authors, the majority being male. Male authors used the constricting sonnet as a respite from the burdensome freedom allowed by free verse epic poetry (233). The male author "free[d] himself by binding himself" (233) in a difficult rhyme scheme because he was jaded by, in Wordsworth's words, the "weight of too much liberty" (qtd. in Hutchinson 199). This burden was the "liberty" allowed in other poetic genres; the privilege to choose when to be constrained in poetry symbolized the male privilege to choose when to be constrained in the everyday world. In the time of the English sonnet's first wave of popularity, the Renaissance, the male was free to work, travel, write, study, and converse as he pleased. However, according to Fried, women were confined with "small room to travel and small room to change the narrative of their lives, already plotted for them as the sex that stay[ed] enclosed at home" (Thesing 233). Since the woman was not accustomed to excessive liberty, the sonnet was no rejuvenating constraint of creativity for her. The sonnet allowed only male authors an abstemious revival because they were the only ones privileged with freedom in other literary outlets. Thus, the sonnet symbolized freedom through constraint for the male while it merely restated the limitations imposed on the female (233).

Similar to **[transition]** Fried's discussion are Stacy Carson Hubbard's comments about gender influences on the sonnet (Freedman 100). Hubbard argues that the traditional Renaissance and Romantic Shakespearean love sonnet gives to males the role of seeking and seducing while it always reduces the female to an object without a voice. If the woman is allowed any expression, her voice is given only when she accepts her male pursuer's advances (104). Hubbard states, "Male desire in the courtly love sonnet was always a masquerade of feminine weakness and sentimentality; wan, beseeching, and consumed by desire, the male lover speaks with the authority of suffering and, perhaps more importantly, with the authority of convention" (113).

The use of the sonnet to suppress females is also discussed later in Debra Fried's "Andromeda Unbound" article. **[Transitional phrase supports the author's position.]** She considers Keats' "If by Dull Rhymes Our English Must Be Chained" (Thesing 240). In this sonnet, English author Keats symbolizes the sonnet as a woman bound by chains (rhymes) and rescued by the author. Since the woman, or sonnet, is sweet only when fettered, the author does not "free" her from her chains. In fact, the author only *rearranges* the shackles (rhymes) and tricks the woman (sonnet) into thinking that she herself fashioned the chains as decorative garlands. The poet crafts the chains, though "even if a poet wishes to bind her with 'garlands of her own' they will be the garlands he has experimentally determined are proper to her, garlands of his own after all," and therefore, they are not the garlands appropriate for her (243). Fried uses this Keats sonnet as a quintessential model of how the traditional male-dominant sonnet treats women: as bound objects of desire or manipulation.

With this highly biased atmosphere surrounding them, it is interesting that Edna St. Vincent Millay chose to write sonnets. **[The paper narrows its focus.]** Many critics dispute the reasons for her choice genre. Biographer Judith Farr argues that Millay submitted to the respected Petrarchan sonnets to control her imagination while prompting her emotional expression (Thesing 230). In "Female Female (sic) Impersonator: Millay and the Theatre of Personality," Susan Gilbert uses Millay's "I Will Put Chaos into Fourteen Lines" to argue Millay's purpose through some of her sonnet-writing: to seduce male readers in the sonnet's octave and then betray them in the following sestet (305). Jane Stanbrough offers another argument as to Millay's choice of genre. Millay presents a woman's "psychological disintegration" through the sonnet because, Stanbrough believes, it is a fitting conductor of feelings regarding the victimization of a woman. In the regulated fourteen lines, Millay symbolizes the female's persistent struggle against boundaries, with the desire to be free contingent with a sense of restriction (227). Quite a different point of view surfaces in Debra Fried's "Andromeda Unbound" article. After extensively describing the gender issues hidden in the traditional sonnet form, Fried sheds light on why Millay chose to write sonnets:

> For a woman writing poetry in the years between the [World W]ars, the brittleness of oaths
> and the shaky fiction of new sexual freedom for women made the sonnet an apt form in which
> to scrutinize the inherited stances of men toward women and poets toward their muses. . . .
> Millay invades the sanctuary of male poetic control with her unsettling formalism. (243)

[Four ellipsis points are used when the quotation ends one complete sentence and begins another.]

Perhaps many or all of these reasons compelled Millay to record her poetry through fourteen carefully crafted lines. **[The paper is driven forward as it reflects the thesis statement.]** Whatever her rationale, Millay at least expressed her method of approaching the sonnet in "I will put Chaos into fourteen lines."

> I will put Chaos into fourteen lines
> And keep him there; and let him thence escape
> If he be lucky; let him twist, and ape
> Flood, fire, and demon– his adroit designs
> Will strain to nothing in the strict confines
> Of this sweet Order, where, in pious rape,
> I hold his essence and amorphous shape,
> Till he with Order mingles and combines.
> Past are the hours, the years, of our duress,
> His arrogance, our awful servitude:
> I have him. He is nothing more nor less
> Than something simple not yet understood;
> I shall not even force him to confess;
> Or answer. I will only make him good.

(Millay, Norma 728) **[Source's full name is used to differentiate between similar names.]**

These words demonstrate that for Millay, sonnet writing is not a brief haven from the "weight of too much liberty." Neither is sonnet writing merely rearranging decorative rhymes on a fettered sonnet-woman, as it is to Keats. Rather, it is a battle for achieving respectable art. Millay attempts to catch the wild animal Chaos and wrestle him--notice that Chaos is male--into a cage of meter and rhythm. According to Fried, Millay's cage for Chaos is not immobilizing with iron bars, but instead, it snares the elusive culprit with flexible tethers. Millay is not ruthless to her prisoner; she forces Chaos's mating with Order only to achieve the greater good of edifying him. Rather than torturing him with stiff rhymes until he releases "something simple," Millay allows Chaos to retain his mystery. She is satisfied that the well-craftedness of the sonnet will suffice in luring Chaos into Order, in transforming regular words into meaningful art (Thesing 237).

Fried offers another insight into "I will put Chaos into fourteen lines," an insight referring to the gender discrimination in the traditional sonnet. She says that this Millay sonnet

> explicitly equates sexual and poetic dominance in its insistence on the control and compression required of the woman poet who seizes upon traditional forms in order to free herself from the forces that would deny her the power to order poetic forms--forces that include traditional male accounts of the need for poetic order. (237-38) **[Block quotation woven into the sentence structure]**

These "traditional male accounts" are what have been previously referred to in mentioning Wordsworth and Keats. Opposing Keats and Wordsworth, Millay tackles the gender issues head-on by treating the sonnet as a conquered male. In "I Will Put Chaos . . ." Keats' sweetly fettered woman has turned around to enslave *him* through rhymes and meter. Millay's approach was shocking and unconventional, to say the least.

In other sonnet sequences, Millay's approach to gender is more subtle but equally, if not more, effective. **[Transitional sentence supporting the outline headings]** Through *Fatal Interview* she attacks the biases by writing a traditional sonnet series about the age-old subject of a love affair. Millay radically twists the perspectives of the seducer and object, though. She characterizes a *female* "initiator, aggressor, and controller as well as victim, sufferer, and survivor" and likewise dumbfounds the expected masculine-feminine perspective (Thesing 211). Millay's female no longer corroborates the English poet Lord Byron's epithet "Man's love is of man's life a thing apart, / 'Tis woman's whole existence–" (qtd. 202). Byron implies that a woman is lost without a man; Edna St. Vincent Millay disagrees. Her raw emotion in *Fatal Interview* initiates the strong-female perspective into the English sonnet sequence, a perspective uncharacteristic of the male-dominated genre (Burch 77-80). Her feminine viewpoint is neither weak nor objectified. Fried claims that Millay is very conscious of how her characterized females and how she herself, as a female poet, are expected to behave in traditional sonnets; and yet she dives into the genre, using the very male-dominant poetics seeking to exclude her in order to gain acceptance into and subtly transform the genre of the sonnet. **[The thesis statement is mirrored here to support the author's position.]**

Millay tackles other gender-related issues in *Sonnets from an Ungrafted Tree*. The bold female speaker in the series has left her husband but returns years later to care for him as he dies. The woman's paramount grief is not that her husband is dying--for him she has no love--but is that she never shared a true love within her marriage. Instead of feigning conventional sadness over losing her spouse, the woman mourns "the domestic tragedy of an action that did not happen" (Thesing 290). Millay captures through the resisting yet dutiful wife the often-ignored depression resulting from an estranged marriage.

Millay's style of writing unconventional sonnets prompted and still prompts varied responses from both her contemporary and posthumous critics. **[Transition situating the paper near the present]** Some pre-1950's critics like John Crowe Ransom dismissed Millay's writing as lacking intellect and complexity (Newcomb 271). Months after Millay's death in 1950 came John Ciardi's article demoting Millay's poetry to immaturity and adolescence (Newcomb 275). These harsh reviews came, not surprisingly, from males. Later criticism from Jane Stanbrough and Stacy Carson Hubbard seems to waver between negative and positive assessment. Stanbrough wrote a 1979 article evaluating Millay's poetry, specifically *Fatal Interview* and *Sonnets from an Ungrafted Tree*, from the perspective that Millay was a deeply troubled woman, insecure and depressed over her vulnerability as a female. Stanbrough demonstrates how many Millay sonnets can be interpreted as expressing such victimized emotion (213-28). In "Love's 'Little Day,'" Stacy Carson Hubbard spends most of her effort praising Millay's sonnets, save those with "a throwaway quality." She notes that "the judgment of Millay's sonnets as logically and verbally thin . . . is not entirely unearned" (Freedman 114). While some of Millay's negative criticism stems from a male-dominant attitude, other reviews like those of Stanbrough and Hubbard are based on studied objections.

While the earlier negative criticism erupted from a few reviewers, **[transition showing contrast]** praise for Millay's sonnets also poured in. As early as 1924, Harriet Monroe declared that Millay's expertise with sonnets was proof of her literary genius (Thesing 136). Allen Tate, in 1931, honored the way Millay's sonnets flow like a smooth machine, guided by a master artisan's hand. He went so far as to recommend her best sonnets against the greatest Shakespearean sequences (64). While some critics disapproved of Millay's abundant literary allusions, Atkins commended her sonnets' clever acknowledgment of both widely recognized and more obscure classic authors. Millay often cited authors like Ovid and Catullus as well as Shakespeare and Wordsworth (Atkins 203).

The abundant list of those contemporaries hailing Millay's sonnets could go on and on. Even in more recent reviews, key critics offer substantiated and convincing arguments in Millay's favor. Robert Johnson thoroughly researches the approach Millay's sonnets take toward Renaissance and Modernistic ideas of time. Through his studies, he concludes that her sonnets both brilliantly converse with and argue against time's power "to limit, to deny, yet also to nurture human understanding . . . of experience." In her sonnets, Millay appears to tussle with time itself in her search for understanding (Freedman 117). Though Johnson hailed Millay's ability to encapsulate the present, fleeting moment of time, Millay had often been criticized as being archaic for writing in the outdated sonnet (123). In "Millay and Modernism," Gilbert Allen scrutinizes this criticism by examining the sonnets' content. He contends that though the sonnet form had grown antiquated and unpopular during her lifetime, Millay integrated progressive and "modern" perspectives into her subject matter. The result was sonnets that "seemed both new *and* eloquent, rather than either genteel or antipoetic . . . . Millay managed to satisfy her audience's demand for the unexpected and for the familiar simultaneously" (Thesing 267). Since some of Millay's most bitter criticism erupted from males, the praise she posthumously receives from both Johnson and Allen is significant.

Edna St. Vincent Millay consistently challenged the gender biases concealed in the traditional sonnet. Many readers during her lifetime enjoyed her poetry for its seemingly light content: themes of politics, time, and love. Others condemned it for the very same reason. Only recently in careful reappraisals of Millay's sonnets have critics discerned the hidden drama underneath her customary themes. **[This sentence makes the conclusion effective and up-to-date.]** Millay was a poet who employed her finest art form to undermine the sonnet's male-dominance that had, for so long, gone unrecognized. **[The conclusive paragraph reiterates the main points without restating them.]**

Works Cited

Atkins, Elizabeth. <u>Edna St. Vincent Millay and Her Times</u>. Chicago: Chicago UP, 1936.

Barnett, Elizabeth. <u>Collected Sonnets of Edna St. Vincent Millay (Revised and Expanded Edition)</u>.

    New York: Harper and Row, 1988.

Brittin, Norman A. <u>Edna St. Vincent Millay</u>. Boston: Twayne, 1982.

Burch, Francis F. "Millay's Not in a Silver Casket Cool with Pearls." <u>Explicator</u> 48.4 (1990): 277-80.

Freedman, Diane P., ed. <u>Millay at 100: A Critical Reappraisal</u>. Carbondale: S. Illinois UP, 1995.

Hutchinson, Thomas, ed. <u>Wordsworth Poetical Works</u>. London: Oxford UP, 1967.

Millay, Norma, ed. <u>Collected Poems: Edna St. Vincent Millay</u>. New York: Harper and Bros., 1956.

Newcomb, John Timberman. "The Woman as Political Poet: Edna St. Vincent Millay and the

    Mid-Century Canon." <u>Criticism</u> 37.2 (1995): 261-77.

"Sonnet." <u>The New Encyclopaedia Britannica: Micropaedia</u>. 15th ed. 1993.

Thesing, William B., ed. <u>Critical Essays on Edna St. Vincent Millay</u>. New York: G.K. Hall, 1993.

RESEARCH LANGUAGE GLOSSARY

Audience—people who hear or read what you have written; sometimes they are the people who have decided what you write, and maybe even the purpose of your writing

Bias—a mental leaning or inclination; partiality; prejudice

Bibliography—a list of the editions, dates, authorship, etc. of books and other writings; a list of sources of information on a given subject, period, etc., or of the literary works of a given author, publisher, etc. See also *working bibliography*.

Card catalogue—an alphabetical card file, as of the books in a library; before computer databases, card catalogues were the main means of locating information stored in a library (See computerized catalog).

CD-ROM—a compact disk that can hold large amounts of information, including moving video images; libraries store vast amounts of information on CD-ROMs

Citation—quoted information from a passage, book, speech, writer, etc.; reference to or mention of by way of example, proof, precedent, etc.

Cognitive Process dimensions—one of the two dimensions that make up the framework for teaching, learning, and assessing (a revision of Bloom's Taxonomy); cognitive process dimensions include remembering, understanding, applying, analyzing, evaluating, and creating

Communication—a giving or exchanging of information, signals, or messages by talk, gestures, writing, etc. or by telephone, telegraph, radio, electronic media, etc.

Computerized catalog—a computerized version of the card catalog; saves space and makes research more efficient; identified book by author, title, or subject, and sometimes by keyword that may appear in the title or even a book's call number; provides the same information as a card catalog: author, title, place of publication, publisher, and special features, including the book's call number which tells you where to find the book in the library

Conclusion—the last division of a discourse, often containing a summary of what went before; the last step in a reasoning process; judgment, decision, or opinion formed after investigation or thought

Dewey Decimal System—a system for book classification in libraries, using three-digit numbers, further extended beyond a decimal point for subclasses; classifies books under ten major headings: general works, philosophy and psychology, religion, social sciences, language, natural sciences and mathematics, technology and applied sciences, fine arts, literature, and geography and history; originated by Melvil Dewey (1851-1931), U. S. librarian and educator

Diction—a manner of expression in words; choice of words; wording; includes good usage, exactness, conciseness (avoiding wordiness and needless repetition), clarity (with articles, pronouns, conjunctions, prepositions, and verbs and their auxiliaries), and completeness (with comparisons and intensifiers)

Draft—a preliminary writing of a work to be completed after revision, editing, and proofreading

Edit—one step in the preparation of an author's works, journals, letters, etc. for publication; usually follows revision or is accomplished simultaneously with revision but before proofreading; to change an original document by adding, deleting, or replacing certain parts

Effective sentences—thoughts expressed correctly and appropriately with attention given to coherence (misplaced parts and dangling modifiers), unity (consistency), subordination and coordination, parallelism, emphasis, and variety, along with the expected attention to fragments, comma splices and fused sentences, adjectives and adverbs, pronouns, and verbs

Electronic databases—large numbers of sources stored in systems accessed by computers; university servers provide access through such databases as ERIC, netLibrary, PsycInfo, etc.; student research can be aided by using Questia.com

Endnotes—the compilation of notes placed as a single group at the end of a chapter or at the end of a paper or book; endnotes lessen the burden of typing the paper; endnotes are related to the paper by inserting a superscripted numeral in the text that corresponds to the number in the endnote

Enthymeme—a type of thesis statement that makes a claim supported with a *because* clause; alerts readers that the writer is going to explain and defend the claim

Essay—a piece of prose writing in which ideas on a single topic are presented, explained, argued, or described in an interesting way; a short literary composition of an analytical or interpretative kind, dealing with its subject usually from a personal point of view or in a limited way

Footnote—a note of comment or reference or an additional comment placed at the bottom of a page and that corresponds to the text by the use of superscript numerals

Format—the shape, size, binding, typeface, paper, and general makeup or arrangement of a book, magazine, journal, etc.

Free write—to write openly and freely on any topic, usually without stopping for a designated period of time; focused free writing is writing openly on a specific topic or idea

Grammar—the study of the structure and features of a language; grammar usually consists of rules and standards that are to be followed to produce acceptable writing and speaking

Hypothesis—a type of thesis statement that sets forth a theory that must be proven in order to be valid

Index—an alphabetical list of names, subjects, etc., (or a list describing the items of a collection) together with the page numbers where they appear in the text, usually placed at the end of a book or other publication; students of research find indexes very valuable for discovering information for their subjects

Integrity—the quality or state of being complete; unbroken condition; wholeness; entirety; the quality or state of being unimpaired; perfect condition; soundness; the quality or state of being of sound moral principle; uprightness, honesty, and sincerity

Introduction—the preliminary section of a piece of writing, usually explaining or defining the subject matter; brings to attention a body of knowledge to be questioned, explored, explained, argued, or described

Knowledge dimensions—one of the two dimensions that make up the framework for teaching, learning, and assessing (a revision of Bloom's Taxonomy); knowledge dimensions include factual knowledge, conceptual knowledge, procedural knowledge, and metacognitive knowledge

Library—a room or public or private institution where a collection of books, periodicals, musical scores, computer databases, etc. is kept for reading or reference in a large systematic arrangement

Library of Congress System—a system for book classification in libraries; classifies books into twenty major groups including general works; philosophy, psychology, and religion; general history; world history; American history; geography and anthropology; social sciences; political science; law; education; music; fine arts; language and literature; science; medicine; agriculture; technology; military science; naval science; bibliography and library science; the public national library in Washington, D. C. established in 1800 by the U. S. Congress and housing one of the largest collections of printed material in the world

Library resource—any thing, person, action, or body of knowledge that one turns to for aid in the discovery of information in the library or database while researching

Manuscript—a book or document written by hand, especially before the invention of printing; a written, typewritten, or computer version of a document or paper, especially an author's copy of his/her work, as submitted to a publisher or printer; writing as distinguished from print

Mechanics—the technical aspects of writing, including spelling, hyphenation, capitals, italics, abbreviations, acronyms, numbers, and document design

On-line—controlled by or connected to another computer or to a network; connected to the Internet or World Wide Web

Outline—a summary of a subject, consisting of a systematic listing of its most important points; an outline for a piece of writing can be formulated with words, phrases, sentences, and even paragraphs; the systematic listing should be parallel in structure

Parenthetical notation—information interjected as qualifying information or explanation; in researched writing this interjected information identifies the source from which the particular information was obtained

Paragraph—a distinct section or subdivision of a paper, chapter, letter, etc., usually dealing with a particular point; it is begun on a new line and is often indented

Paraphrase—a rewording of the meaning expressed in something spoken or written (compare with summary)

Periodical—a journal, magazine, or other literary work that is published at regular intervals, as weekly, monthly, etc.

Plagiarize—to take the ideas, writings, words, etc., from another and pass them off as one's own

Print—an edition of a paper, book, etc. which has undergone all the processes connected with publishing the paper, i.e. composition, drafting, revision, editing, proofreading and then using a computer (and typesetting and presswork with book publication) to produce the readable text

Proofread—to read and mark corrections on a piece of writing; to test or try the truth, worth, quality, validity of a piece of writing

Publish—to make publicly known; to announce, proclaim, divulge, or promulgate; to issue a printed work to the public

Punctuation—the act, practice, or system of using standardized marks in writing and printing to separate sentences or sentence elements or to make the meaning clearer, including the comma, the semicolon, the apostrophe, quotation marks, the period, the exclamation mark, the colon, the dash, the *en* dash, the *em* dash, parentheses, brackets, the slash, and ellipsis points.

Quality source—the degree of excellence with a thing possesses; in references, the degree of validity and integrity that backs up the hypothesis or statements

Reference—an indication, as in a book or article, of some other work or passage to be consulted; the mark or sign, as a number, letter, or symbol, directing the reader to a footnote or endnote or the Works Cited; a work that is used or consulted to get information, as in research

Reflection—the fixing of the mind on some subject; serious thought; contemplation leading to or considering thoughts, ideas, or conclusions

Relevance—implies close logical relationship with, and importance to, the matter under consideration

Research—careful, systematic, patient study and investigation in some field of knowledge, undertaken to discover or establish facts or principles

Research Portfolio—a collection of the pieces of works used in the research process, organized according to specification, then compiled, labeled, dated, and presented by the researcher to the audience

Revise—to change a piece of writing to improve it in style or content

Source—see reference; the place where the reference originates

Style—a manner or mode of expression in language, as distinct from the ideas expressed; way of using words to express thoughts; specific or characteristic manners of expression, execution, construction, or design; distinction, excellence, originality, and character in any form of artistic or literary expression

Style manuals—books consisting of examples or rules of style

Summary—a brief statement or account covering the substance or main points (compare with paraphrase)

Thesis—a statement of the purpose, intent, or main idea of a piece of writing

Transitions—words, phrases, sentences, or paragraphs, that help tie writing together

Voice—the angle from which a paper is written; usually identified by first person or third person

Working bibliography—a complete listing of all editions, dates, authorship, etc. of books and other writings used in a particular piece of writing, i.e. research writing; a complete list of all sources of information on a given subject, period, etc. or of the literary works of a given author, publisher, etc., used in a particular piece of writing, i.e. researched writing

Works Cited—a listing of reference materials actually used in the research paper, including any reference made in general in the context of the paper; includes all publication data on every source used so as to give all scholars in the field a consistent way to consult the sources (compare with bibliography and working bibliography)

Write—to be the author or composer of a piece of writing; to draw up, communicate, entitle, designate, underwrite, record, etc. in writing

BIBLIOGRAPHY

Anderson, Lorin W., David R. Krathwohl, Peter W. Airasian, Kathleen A. Cruikshank, Richard E. Mayer, Paul R. Pintrich, James Raths, and Merlin C. Wittrock, eds. <u>A Taxonomy for Learning, Teaching, and Assessing: A Revision of Bloom's Taxonomy of Educational Objectives</u>. New York: Longman, 2001. (WEB: <u>http://www.ablongman.com</u>)

Bede, The Venerable. <u>The Ecclesiastical History of the English Nation</u>. New York: Dent & Sons Ltd., 1927.

Bell, Debra. <u>The Ultimate Guide to Homeschooling, the 2001 Edition</u>. Nashville: T. Nelson, 2001.

Brengle, Richard L. <u>Arthur: King of Britain</u>. New York: Appleton-Century-Crofts, 1964. <u>Chicago Manual of Style</u>. The Fifteenth Edition. Chicago: U of Chicago P, 2003.

Entwistle, William J. <u>Arthurian Legend in the Literatures of the Spanish Peninsula</u>. New York: E. P. Dutton & Co., 1925.

Farris, Michael P. <u>The Home Schooling Gather: How You Can Play a Decisive Role in Your Child's Success.</u> Nashville: Broadman & Holman, 2001.

Farris, Vickie, and Jayne Farris Metzgar. <u>A Mom Just Like You: The Home Schooling Mother</u>. Nashville: Broadman & Holman, 2002.

Field, Christine M. <u>Homeschooling the Challenging Child: A Practical Guide</u>. Nashville: Broadman & Holman: 2005.

Gardner, Howard. <u>Multiple Intelligences: The Theory in Practice, A Reader</u>. New York: Basic Books,1993.

Gibaldi, Joseph. <u>MLA Handbook for Writers of Research Papers</u>, Sixth Edition. New York: MLA of America, 2004.

Giles, J. A., ed. <u>Six Old English Chronicles: Ethelwerd's Chronicles, Asser's Life of Alfred, Geoffrey of Monmouth's British History, Gildas, Nennius, and Richard of Cirencester</u>. London: George Bell & Sons, 1896.

Green, Sharon Weiner, and Ira K Wolf. <u>How to Prepare for the New SAT</u>. 22nd ed. New York: Barron's Educational Series, 2005.

Harris, Gregg. <u>The Christian Home School</u>. Brentwood, TN: Wolgemuth & Hyatt, 1988.

Hendricks, Howard G. <u>Teaching to Change Lives.</u> Portland: Multonomah and Walk Thru the Bible, 1987.

Hodges, John C., Winifred Bryan Horner, Suzanne Strobeck Webb, and Robert Keith Miller. Harbrace College Handbook, Revised Thirteenth Edition with 1998 MLA Manual Updates. New York: Harcourt, 1998.

Hughes, R., and M. Perry-Jenkins. "Social Class Issues in Family Life Education." Family Relations, 45.2 (1996):175-182.

Kaplan Test Preparation and Admissions. The New SAT Critical Reading Workbook. New York: Simon & Schuster, 2004.

Klicka, Christopher. The Heart of Home Schooling: Teaching & Living What Really Matters. Nashville: Broadman & Holman, 2002.

Lester, James D., Sr., and James D. Lester, Jr. Writing Research Papers: A Complete Guide. New York: Longman, 2005.

Loberger, Gordon, and Kate Shoup Welsh. Webster's New World English Grammar Handbook. IN: Wiley Pub, 2002.

McGoldrick, M. "Belonging and Liberation." In Re-visioning Family Therapy: Race, Culture, and Gender in Clinical Practice. Ed. M. McGoldrick. New York: Guilford Press, 1998. 55-70.

Moss, Sheila E. Some Influences of the Arthurian Legends on English and Spanish Literature. Murfreesboro: MTSU Press, 1971.

Nichols, M. and R Schwartz. Family Therapy: Concepts and Methods. 6th ed. Boston: Allyn & Bacon, 2004.

Official SAT Study Guide for the New SAT. New York: College Board, 2004.

Sabin, William A. The Gregg Reference Manual, Ninth Edition. Glencoe McGraw-Hill: 2001.

Schultz, Glen. Kingdom Education: God's Plan for Educating Future Generations. Nashville: LifeWay Press: 2002.

Schultz, Ivan. "Elizabethan Chivalry and The Faerie Queene's Feast." Modern Language Notes, 50 (1935): 158-161.

Sebranek, Patrick, Verne Meyer, and Dave Kemper. Writer's Inc. Write for College: A Student Handbook. Wilmington: Great Source Education Group, Houghton, 1997.

Vitz, Paul C. Censorship: Evidence of Bias in Our Children's Textbooks. Ann Arbor: 1986.

Williams, John, ed. Annals Cambriae. London: Longman, 1860.

LaVergne, TN USA
16 July 2010
189678LV00001B/14/P

9 780805 443646